Counselling skills
FOR COMPLE
THERAPISTS

12.99
99
8

Counselling skills
FOR COMPLEMENTARY THERAPISTS

Rosie March-Smith

Open University Press

Open University Press
McGraw-Hill Education
McGraw-Hill House
Shoppenhangers Road
Maidenhead
Berkshire
England
SL6 2QL

email: enquiries@openup.co.uk
world wide web: www.openup.co.uk

and Two Penn Plaza, New York, NY 10121–2289, USA

First published 2005

A catalogue record of this book is available from the British Library

ISBN-13: 978 0335 21122 7 (pb)   978 0335 21123 4 (hb)
ISBN-10: 0 335 21122 4 (pb)   0 335 21123 2 (hb)

Library of Congress Cataloging-in-Publication Data
CIP data applied for

Typeset by RefineCatch Limited, Bungay, Suffolk
Printed in the UK by Bell & Bain Ltd, Glasgow

Contents

Acknowledgements

Many people have helped me in the preparation of this book. In particular, my thanks to Prof. Michael Jacobs, who encouraged me to consider tackling it in the first place and for his elegant editing. I would like to thank also friends and colleagues who gave so generously of their time and interest: Prof. Roger Baker, Thelma Buckley, Dr. Adrian Clarke, Isobel Cosgrove, Zofia Dymitr, Dr. Dina Glouberman, Katharine Jenking, Maureen Leigh, Dr. J.R. Millenson, Dr. Denise Peerbhoy, Susanne Preiss, Brigitte Scott, Dr. Roy Welford, Jacqueline Wood and Dr. Roger Woolger.

The Avenue Clinic of Complementary Medicine in Yeovil, Somerset, has provided me with the best possible group of therapists to contribute their thoughts and experience for some of my research. Warmest thanks, therefore, to Richard Bertschinger, Elizabeth Clayton, Ned Reiter and Jane Robinson – all of whom offered a wealth of observations, personal insights and professionally helpful material.

Nearer to home, my loving thanks to Vivienne Ruckert and R.G.S. for their own special contributions; Flora Myer; my son James for his invaluable I.T. support, always available to de-mystify and respond to S.O.S. calls for electronic help; and my younger son Matt, for his equally constant encouragement and interest.

To Derek Smith, ever-supportive, patient and practical, my love also and deep gratitude for seeing me through difficult but exciting times: the indexing not least of them.

Foreword

Many training courses for those wishing to become complementary therapists do not provide the opportunities to develop and practice the counselling skills needed to prepare graduates adequately for the psychotherapeutic processes occurring within patient-practitioner interactions. The necessary theme of practitioner development skills within courses should extend throughout the provision embedding counselling skills, and in particular draw on experiences and incidents from clinical practice. So much is to be gained from the evaluation of cases across the entire spectrum of therapies and healthcare professions. Some quality courses ensure that practitioner and counselling skills are developed within multidisciplinary groups. In this way, 'critical incidents' and the transferability of the insights gained are clearly recognized, preparing practitioners for participation in the multidisciplinary supervision that may be a requirement in a future integrated healthcare system.

By drawing on numerous examples from widely diverse therapies, Rosie March-Smith's book is relevant to all complementary therapists and to practitioners in other healthcare professions. In addition, no matter how much previous training or experience the complementary therapist has had in counselling skills, the cases included in her book provide invaluable illustrations of concepts and demonstrate the application of theory to practice. For all those in practice as complementary therapists, this book provides the opportunity to reflect on how counselling skills enable practitioners to respond appropriately in consultations. The cases cited illustrate the importance of the establishment of boundaries, of knowing where to stop in order to help prevent making mistakes, and when to refer.

Rosie March-Smith's emphasis on the need to encompass the body-mind-soul aspects of healing is a valuable reminder of the importance of holistic or naturopathic approaches to treatment. Other themes within the book further illustrate the principles of naturopathy. These include insights into what may be described as the holistic therapeutic encounter, in which the patient is viewed as an individual; the recognition of the importance of the healing power of nature and the life force; and an acknowledgement of the need to empower the patient.

The strength of the book comes from its exploration of the main aspects of counselling through cases drawn from the author's wide experience of complementary therapies. Her insightful chapters on 'Perils and Psychic Protection' and 'Dealing with Difficulties' (topics rarely included in texts on counselling skills) are of great value to the holistic practitioner, in particular those working as sole practitioners or where there is no supportive network of colleagues. Moreover, the exploration of the principles and practice of reflective practice and the importance of supervision are reminders of how significant these aspects have now become as components of the continuing professional development requirements of many of the professional bodies.

While reading this book, I was constantly aware of two observations. The first: 'If only such an applied text on counselling skills had been available 15 years ago, when I was undergoing my training as an osteopath and naturopath!' The second, that the material is relevant not only to complementary therapists but to all other healthcare practitioners, for whom enhanced counselling skills would maximize the therapeutic interaction within any consultation.

BRIAN ISBELL
Head of the Department of Complementary Therapies,
University of Westminster, London

Chapter 1

Patients deserve more than sympathy

The use of counselling skills in holistic practice, though not under that name, might be said to go back a long, long way. Fifty thousand years ago, a Neanderthal man's body was buried in what is now northern Iraq and archeologists unearthing him discovered a variety of medicinal herbs surrounding the skeleton. A poignant sign perhaps that, while their therapeutic value may have failed in life, they were to take care of his welfare in the next world. Why they were so placed cannot, of course, be proved: but the presence of healing herbs clearly held significance to that prehistoric community. From this we might allow ourselves to guess that some form of discussion, an intimate meeting between patient and herbalist, preceded his final hours. Crude, maybe, but possibly true.

We do know that acupuncture was practised in China six thousand years ago; that Persians, Egyptians, Greeks and Romans all consulted their healer priests throughout the millenia separating these giant civilizations. It would be hard to imagine that in those one-to-one meetings – at some level so comparable to today's therapy room – meaningful communication was not exchanged; that the patient was not encouraged to talk so that the healer could listen and make helpful interventions to draw out as full a diagnostic a picture as possible.

If we scan this vast timescale – taking in Sumerian, shamanic societies in the Americas, the so-called less civilized peoples across the globe such as the aboriginals, African medicine men and the tribal wise women – we are struck by the significance of it all. Counselling, in one sense, might actually have had as its birthplace ancient Mesopotamia (northern Iraq) at the time of Neanderthal man 50,000 years ago, or maybe even earlier. The problems of disease were probably based on simple story lines where survival from day to day formed the main focus. As mankind evolved, a place for the healer priest was heralded throughout the pre-Christian world, a spiritual companion to accompany the traveller as he or she sought the body–mind–spirit connection. Few would argue that this is not unlike the remit of twenty-first century holistic practitioners.

Fear, anger and sadness may have been integral to the somatic and other symptoms experienced by prehistoric men and women presenting themselves for healing, and we might assume that those who practised the arts were, within the obvious limitations of primitive society, skilled at their job. Indeed, the simplicity of life then, compared with our own complex, crowded existence, may have provided a less confused backdrop against which the practitioner worked, where qualities such as intuition, holding ability and insight may well have flowed more instinctively than they do today. It is not new to suggest here that modern medicine has lost some of the delicacy, the finely tuned 'bedside' approach enjoyed in the past, even by our own grandparents.

They did not, however, benefit from our powerful drugs: modern technology saves more lives than ever before and we should not complain if one has virtually supplanted the other. But we do need to face the consequences of this advance and of this state of affairs. Psychological distress can be a killer too, despite the plethora of drugs now available – and, indirectly, through its insidious impact on the body. Iatrogenic (doctor-induced) illness is, paradoxically, responsible for a significant percentage of patients in hospital care at any one time, where prescribed drugs' side-effects have caused additional suffering. It would seem that the allopathic world has lost touch with the Greek philosopher Plato's belief that 'the cure of the part should not be attempted without treatment of the whole. No attempts should be made to cure the body without the soul, and if the head and body are to be healthy you must begin by curing the mind, for this is the great error of our day in the treatment of the human body that physicians first separate the soul from the body.' Plato's words have as much relevance now as they ever did, though it would be unfair to suggest that all our doctors and consultants are guilty of splitting the body from mind and soul, addressing only the parts. Yet such people are rare; they are exceptions and not the rule.

Twenty-first century crises

Luxury, rather than the struggle for survival, has become a key factor in the unprecedented levels of stress experienced by westerners today. Having so much choice, too much uncertainty in securing the means to achieve that choice, conflict in domestic and work relationships – seedbeds for loneliness and depression – all contribute to the difficulties facing us now. Psychologist and author Oliver James (quoted in Owen 2003: 7) believes that higher divorce rates, broken homes and a declining role for religion have left people disorientated: 'There is a very strong case for the proposition that people are working too hard for their own good. People genuinely are mentally worse off than they used to be. There are three times as many depressed people now as in the Fifties.'

The growth of complementary therapies to meet demand is unequivocal. Psychological trauma is at its most concentrated; we are suffering from overload of one kind or another and we need a safe place in which we may tell our story. Long waits for professional allopathic appointments, disenchantment with dehumanizing contact with hospital or surgery staff (hard-pressed themselves) continue to feed a nationwide hunger for help of a different quality.

Perhaps precisely because we have arrived at this place – blessed with technological marvels, yet short on listening time – more and more patients are turning to complementary practitioners for their emotional well-being, in tandem with seeking symptom relief when allopathic medicine has failed or is preferred by them. Since practitioners are part of the same population, we must accept that they too have been affected by the stress of living in a crowded world. As psychotherapist Andrew Samuels (2003: xi) points out, we live in 'a world starved of, and looking for, authentic relating'.

Practitioners themselves have problems and they too work in this starved world. More troubles lie ahead if they are unaware of such neediness: and this can prove a serious block to the healing process of others, for however strongly they may feel called to heal and have a sense of unlimited amounts of sympathy for all-comers, however much they believe they can rely upon their own sound sense and personal experience to help their patients, it is unlikely this will be enough. Indeed, there can be dangers in holding to these personal views if they do not have a framework of professionally drawn discipline to contain them. So, when an unskilled therapist cries, 'I know just how you're feeling – my dog died last week, on the very day you say your mother died and I'm feeling really dreadful, too . . .', we have the making of a serious breakdown in patient-healer trust. If desolate grief about a lost parent is, apparently, comparable to a pet dying – however valued and loved – then a therapeutic relationship is unlikely to continue. The practitioner may genuinely have empathized with her client, but blind to the crassness of her response and the damaging results, she would have missed her opportunity to hold the moment where it belonged, with the patient.

In this case, the bereaved person might well feel some obligation to move in and take care of the healer. At some unconscious level the therapist pet owner is abusing the situation to seek relief for her own misery. Put another way, we are looking at a classic example of neurosis left unattended: the practitioner is ignorant of her process, of the necessity for her inner world to be explored and to become clearer. That exploration must be done out of working hours, and not at the emotional expense of her patient. This is professional betrayal on the part of the practitioner and yet she could very well argue she was helping her client feel heard, that she was showing the bereaved person her distress had been understood, even shared. This is a mistake many therapists make, maintaining that personal revelation can help along the healing process. And the problem here is that it can indeed do that, but only sometimes. A fine line divides the crass response and the sensitive, creative one and it is actually quite hard to define the difference. Let acupuncturist Jane Robinson explain:

> The trouble is, one person might respond well with the dead dog sharing, and another would be furious at this

intervention. If I felt I had blundered because I sensed their emotional withdrawal at my response, I might have added something like, 'I do realize you are going through a bereavement much tougher than my loss'. In building up a relationship with the patient, it's important to identify where they are coming from, talking the same language. Above all, to give the *patient* recognition.

(personal communication)

In another example where inappropriate material offered by the practitioner can hinder the work, one client attending a community clinic for an aromatherapy massage found herself silenced by the shocking (and lengthy) story from a practitioner who had recently lost her daughter. Denise Peerbhoy (2002: 93) reports: 'This lady did not feel she could say anything, in fact she implied a sense of powerlessness, indicating the only thing she could do was not return. At a following visit to the clinic [for a different treatment], the service user was relieved to find that the practitioner was in a better state . . . but she still held her view about it having a negative impact for her.'

Inappropriate disclosure has its pitfalls, as we can see. There are other interventions equally damaging to the patient–practitioner alliance: omnipotence might be one of them. A newly qualified hypnotherapist whose client had just reported a satisfactory outcome to his quest to stop smoking, beamed – I was told – with a sense of accomplishment and then announced: 'I can help you with all other issues that may be troubling you.' It is a wise person who promises nothing and who realizes their professional limitations. Consider the catastrophic possibilities for an anxious new client who heard this observation made by a reflexologist as she completed relaxation work on a foot: 'You seem to have some disturbance in your liver area. Is there any liver, or pancreatic cancer in your family history? Oh, there is? Never mind, perhaps you won't get it. If I were you, though, I'd put myself on a carrot diet. Just a hunch, but my friends tell me my intuition is usually spot on.' Her reflexology diagnosis may have been spot on in detecting disturbance, but everything else she said is unprofessional and an illustration of unskilled communication. We can see that her rush to be recognized as clever was paramount, regardless of the effect her insight would have upon her patient: another example of consulting room betrayal.

The dangers in unskilled interventions

Counselling skills lie in listening, in recognizing where and where not to go, and in holding the patient in a safe emotional place. Any intervention or chance remark that interferes with these fundamental requirements can seriously jeopardize the relationship between healer and patient. Imposing personal judgements upon anyone in the vulnerable position, whether by subtle suggestion, fervent conviction, or messages from the spirit world (or possibly all three), is also bad practice. Sadly, it happens.

Homeopath Zofia Dymitr points out the downside in what she calls 'bit part training' and adopted spirituality in many of the alternative world's healing services. She cites a New Age worker who purported to channel messages for her clients, one of whom suffered from allergies and was an asthma patient of Dymitr's. The client was visited at his home by the New Age worker who, on seeing the blankets on a bed, declared he must get rid of these, or he would die in six months. 'I telephoned my protest that this was utterly unprofessional conduct,' said Dymitr. 'The worker's response was: "I wouldn't say it if I hadn't channelled this information." This is hardly responsible behaviour, and yet the person spoke as if it was the last word on the matter' (personal communication).

A working knowledge of counselling skills can be a potent tool in drawing out the whole picture to help practitioners offer the best treatment. Such skills can also play a vital part in safeguarding against bad practice as in the cases cited above. Medical herbalist Ned Reiter holds the view that to be under-skilled is dangerous, not least because what he calls advice dispensing might open up a can of worms. He told me:

> Western herbalists tend to use a physiological approach, but detailed questioning can open up whole areas of personal and interpersonal situations. Almost by accident, they may find themselves in situations where counselling is occurring at some level, but they do need to recognise what is going

on. If psycho-emotional problems are the primary cause of a patient's illness, then the skill lies in identifying this and suggesting they move on to a therapist. Our brief with patients isn't overt counselling, it's more a development to try to understand the person as a whole, not just a set of symptoms. There's no clearly defined line, however, between the psycho-emotional and the physical diagnosis. The presenting problem, let's say athlete's foot, can suddenly get forgotten if in our talking together the patient moves towards a painful memory from her childhood. One has to be careful not to get carried away. Knowing where to stop, being clear about what may be happening, is an essential part of this.

(personal communication)

Reiter sees counselling skills not only as an adjunct to successful treatment but as an essential part of proper practice. It teaches us what to do, but more importantly, it helps to prevent mistakes. 'Avoiding wading in, stirring things up, being prescriptive, these are all areas that need our careful attention. An unskilled practitioner might easily say, on hearing about a destructive relationship with a partner, "He sounds a horrible man, you should leave him." This is not the right way. Better to suggest the names of a few good counsellors or psychotherapists and make sure the patient doesn't leave the consulting room with their head and heart emotionally ripped open.'

Possessing counselling skills and being a counsellor are fundamentally different, as Reiter reminds us, and practitioners need to recognize that difference, not stepping outside their own area of expertise. It is vital that the patient's trust remains with the practitioner. Reiter again: 'Realising what's dynamite, in emotional terms, is skilful, and being careful with that material is crucial. For example, a soldier needs to know about mine-fields to avoid getting blown up, but he leaves mine clearance to the experts. In other words, stop getting into areas that belong to the fully trained counsellor.'

The need for humility is central to good practice and, as we have already seen, the lack of it (as in the newly qualified hypnotherapist, puffed up with self-importance) is potentially risky. Many people make an appointment to see a complementary practitioner because they feel the need for help of some kind, even though they may not have been able to recognize what kind of help that should be. This is where the unskilled therapist can have a field day: once the psycho-emotional material pours out, in that intimate and (it is to be hoped) confidential environment, the temptation to adopt the role of Great Healer in all respects can, for some practitioners, prove irresistible.

Transference and counter-transference

Let us now look at a more subtle form of this temptation. We might replace the words Great Healer with Good Father, or Good Mother, understanding that there is a similarity with that role of a caring, attentive parent offering, seemingly, endless time for this needy child: someone to take away the hurt, effectively to 'kiss it better', to murmur reassuring words and to make the consulting room seem just like a cosy room at home from their childhood. The patient, unaware of what is really being acted out in their unconscious world, merely feels relaxed and pleased to have made this appointment. What is actually happening, if this longing for a loving parent is intense enough, is what is called transference on to the practitioner: that is, transferring their feelings from childhood as if they were relevant to the here and now. Whether the patient experienced loving parenting, or whether the lack of it created their unconscious longing for it, is not what we need discuss here. Suffice to say that, despite all appearances to the contrary, this person is at some level reliving their actual or fantasized relationship with their mother or father. Let us imagine, say, a retired civil servant, presenting with stiff and painful joints, his medical diagnosis of irreparable wear and tear damage long established. Remember the triggers: safe, intimate setting, someone on hand to make them feel better. In psychological terms, these are all cues for that interesting, powerful dynamic called transference.

The practitioner, in turn (unless they have identified and inwardly acknowledged their own counter-transference), can bask in this warm, devoted atmosphere and at best believe they must be working well today or, at worst, feel certain of their omnipotence. To the initiated, awareness of this omnipotent sense is a warning sign; they will understand and work with the significance of their counter-transferences, that is, their own feelings about the other person. For example, they might ask, 'Why am I wanting to make him magically well, when I know his arthritis is too far gone?'

Understanding transference and counter-transference can be useful in the therapeutic alliance. It can open up a whole new dimension to the healing environment, if only in the benign guise of child and parent together. Hillman, cited by Hawkins and Shohet (2000: 13), suggests that counter-transference is there from the beginning, 'since some unconscious call in me impels me to do this work. I may bring to my work a need to redeem the wounded child, so that every person who comes to me for help is my own hurt wounded childhood needing its wounds bound up by good parental care. This same parent–child archetype may also affect us, for instance, in the need to correct and punish an entire generation, its ideals and values. My needs are never absent . . . Just as the person who comes to me needs me for help, I need him to express my ability to give help.'

Gestalt psychotherapist Petruska Clarkson (1989: 101) asserts that counter-transference can be destructive when based on the counsellor's own unfinished business. Counsellor or holistic practitioner, the rules are the same. 'In this way it can be the counsellor's contribution to the lack of genuine here-and-now contact with a client . . . [she] may also experience emotions, attitudes and impulses toward the client which are similar to those experienced by significant people from the client's past, for example the urge to reject them in the same way that a hostile parent once did.'

Regression: potentials and pitfalls

It should not be demeaning to a patient sometimes to be seen as a vulnerable person, longing for gentle caring: that can prove a creative part of the healing process just as counsellors and psychotherapists know within the more lengthy work they face with their clients. Essentially, the intimacy and regressive potential in this contact have a valuable place if the unconscious material surfaces and the practitioner is aware of it. It does not always happen and it should never be sought. The psyche is not to be tampered with.

Consider the negative implications in the following case, where a hypnotist had deliberately regressed a client to levels where she believed she was watching scenes from previous lifetimes. The client reports: 'I saw myself in a visualization as a housewife in ancient Greece, buying vegetables in the market square; then as a 9-year-old girl from the Middle Ages, carried off screaming by a horseman; finally, as a Victorian maid. All these images left me profoundly shocked and I was dumbstruck at the sheer reality of what I had seen.' Instead of staying silent and simply holding the moment while the hugeness of the impact had a chance to be absorbed, the hypnotist surged in as if eager to demonstrate how perceptive he was, asking, 'Do you know what the significance is about your being female in these memories? I mean, what have you been avoiding, sticking with the same gender life after life? Do you hate men?'

This practitioner was brutal, both in taking control of an extremely delicate stage in the client's process, but also in expecting her to unravel countless layers from some mysterious depths in her psyche. That could and should take many more sessions, preferably with a competent hypnotist, experienced in such specialist work. The issue here is not about reincarnation, fact or fantasy. It is about paying attention to what is happening to the client. The visions may have been accurate; they may have been simply symbols – like a dream – for how the client views herself; and yes, they may have revealed a current hatred or fear of men. Whatever the case, the practitioner moved in insensitively, prematurely and certainly out of his depth.

The parental metaphor

Recognizing when the psyche has sent a message is certainly not meddling, but it clearly calls for careful, supportive responses. Perhaps the message means noticing and working with the emotional hurts of yesteryear. There is no harm in acknowledging these, possibly in gently pursuing leads offered, thus providing the patient with a sense of relief that someone is finally taking time to listen and sympathize, just as a good parent would do.

However, to the uninitiated practitioner, flattered by the full-on volume of approval and gratitude, obvious dangers lurk.

Hubris takes over, a swelling up of pride that they have done so much good; but with it, unfortunately, no awareness that the patient will probably keep the volume turned on fully for months, maybe years to come. This is not psychologically healthy. No one should depend too long on the services of a practitioner, unless there is sound reason to continue treatment. Just as in the talking treatments, clients are required to wean themselves off dependence and learn, possibly for the first time in their lives, to walk away from 'home' as autonomous human beings. This does not mean, obviously, that there is any limit to the timescale over which the patient sees the practitioner; it does suggest, however, that this particular phase in the relationship needs to move on once it has fulfilled its therapeutic purpose in providing a parental haven.

Naturally, there are dangers in the parental metaphor. Mitchell and Cormack (1998: 111) agree that treatment may at times and in part mirror the process of growing up. They stress that this is only in the context of two experienced people bringing together their different understandings, knowledge and skills to try to solve a problem.

> If this is ignored, then patients run the risk of being disrespected, patronized, belittled and abused. Since the parental metaphor is dominant in our paternalistic culture, it is easy to see the risk of the patient being maintained in a position where 'parent' (doctor, therapist, practitioner) knows best and where his own knowledge and skills are underplayed . . . Complementary practitioners (their emphasis on the patient's own healing power notwithstanding) run as much risk of treating their patients this way as more orthodox practitioners, especially if complementary medicine continues its current move towards more regulated professional status.

Negative transference

What if the patient transfers their negative feelings – their frustration and rage at earlier bad parenting – on to the hapless practitioner? We must consider not only the plight of an abused patient, in the context of power and subtle control, but realize that healers, too, might be on the receiving end of abuse. An angry patient, fuming about their treatment, can be extremely daunting. As Hawkins and Shohet (2000: 14) offer: 'It seems so unfair to be told that one is cold, rigid or misusing power. The temptations are either to alter one's behaviour to be more "pleasing", to counter-attack subtly or otherwise, or stop working with the person for "plausible" reasons. The ingratitude is sometimes hard to accept. We may find ourselves thinking ". . . after all I've done for you", words which we heard from a parent or teacher, and which we promised never to repeat.'

Perhaps the only truly effective way to be clear of feeling this kind of response is (as any psychotherapist trained in a psychodynamic discipline will confirm) to have experienced a fair amount of personal therapy oneself. Through this, we learn about the value of non-attachment, to see that we may have an investment in playing the good parent, being overly sympathetic, warm and caring. And an investment, too, in avoiding being challenged, for somehow failing the patient, not making them better or, possibly, even deserving some of the charges hurled by the angry customer. To quote once more Hawkins and Shohet (2000: 9–10): 'The idea that we are helpers as opposed to a channel for help is a dangerous one. We want the praise for the success, but not the blame for the failure . . . It is hard really to accept the possibility of being only the vehicle of help. Yet this acceptance is the only way to get off the roundabout of being addicted to praise and fearful of blame, and to stop ourselves lurching wildly between impotence and omnipotence.'

The need for better practice

To find one explanation for the less-than-perfect interventions cited in the examples above, we need look no further than the mushrooming over the past twenty years or so of all the alternative therapies on offer. Some practitioners in those early years had sparse training (weekend workshop 'diploma' courses are still notoriously in our memory) and, more importantly in the context of this book, no counselling training to support the professional work. This is not to blame those first agencies – we all have to start somewhere – but merely to point out and celebrate that we have reached a stage where this lack has been, or is now being, addressed. Fortunately, accrediting bodies in all the major areas of alternative or complementary healing increasingly include teaching counselling skills on their syllabus. Where once we were lucky to see a practitioner with more than a few hours' counselling training under their belt, we now might hope to meet as a matter of course those whose learning embraces at the very least listening and interactive skills. But there is still a long way to go. There is an urgent need to ensure that practitioners throughout the vast panoply of complementary healing arts learn more than the basics of counselling.

Hands-on work in tandem with the careful use of talking treatment skills can be an immensely powerful combination and there can be no doubt that their joint value will be proved more and more so in the twenty-first century.

Summary

The use of counselling is an ancient skill, where attention to the body–mind–soul aspect of healing has probably been integral to all encounters. There is a need for a return to that holistic approach today, as mainstream complementary practitioners already increasingly realize. However, knowing how to listen professionally, how to avoid inappropriate interventions, how best to draw out a patient's trust the better to treat him or her, is not yet fully appreciated by everyone in this field, perhaps because the main thrust in alternative, or complementary, therapy training has been on healing. Body and soul are fully acknowledged: yet the mind seems, somewhat surprisingly for holistic workers, to have taken a back seat. Psychological realities such as transference and counter-transference in the patient–healer alliance need to be identified, and they should form a significant role in the practitioner's 'tool kit'. These more complex areas in the consulting room are important, and they can and should be learned if we are to go forward under the holistic banner. The significance of these dynamics, and of other aspects of the therapeutic relationship from the moment the patient walks into the room, are discussed further in the next chapter.

Chapter 2

Why counselling needs rules

Complementary practice holds an unusual place in the field where the use of counselling skills can be beneficial. With the possible exception of the general practitioner's consulting room (although time constraints there enforce a different caveat), the majority of professional settings, from teaching to ambulance driving, make time for counselling, even in its covert form of a friendly chat. Complementary healers, on the other hand, must learn to juggle two disciplines in one sitting; indeed, for homeopaths and herbalists particularly, exploratory talk forms an integral part of their search for the fuller picture. Throughout the session, they must be alert to subtexts of one hue or another.

Nevertheless, all holistic practitioners need to assess what is really going on, what treatment is appropriate, what to say and what not to say. An acupuncturist will let her needles do the healing, but her verbal skills can steer her more precisely to decide, in tandem with information she gleans from the pulses, where best to place those needles. As Mitchell and Cormack (1998: 2) confirm: 'Psychological or interpersonal processes inevitably form part of all treatment encounters and these processes can be used to the patient's advantage.' Yet patients who come for complementary health care are not necessarily asking for, or wanting, counselling; according to Mitchell and Cormack, many may have actively chosen not to engage directly with psychological or interpersonal issues, and those authors believe that choice must be respected. Overt counselling has to be by consensual agreement. Some patients are already aware of a connection between their illness and their emotional distress and may seem eager to explore those links with the help of a skilled listener. Others, on the other hand, could reject the notion that there is any link between the two. For them, the word 'psychosomatic' holds fear of moral weakness or imaginary illness. As Millenson (1995: 133) points out: 'Pushing an unwilling or unprepared patient to accept a relation between the mind and body that he does not feel or dares not consider will be fruitless and probably counterproductive.' Small wonder, then, that alternative therapists may encounter stiff resistance to even the most gentle intervention.

One cranial osteopath offers some insight into this. Elizabeth Clayton describes a woman in her forties, presenting with back pain and asthma. She had a large, deep scar on her chest which, she explained, had been caused by a road accident when she was 3 years old. Clayton began treatment first by relaxing the thorax area, which she found to be extremely restricted. It felt to her as if this restriction was chronic, probably linked with the road accident. The patient responded well, and in time reported great improvement in her breathing, so much so that (with her doctor's agreement) she slowly reduced her bronchodilator drug. But the relationship with her husband had meanwhile deteriorated, he having angrily refused her request for a financially secure separation. 'Soon she was back up to full-strength medication again, telling me she felt trapped. I asked an open question like, "Have you been able to talk to anyone about this?" and she replied, "Yes, but not with the right person" (meaning her husband). In my hands, I felt she was utterly locked. She is such a private person, I didn't feel it appropriate to pry: I had done all I could. In time, she found the courage to seek out a counsellor to work specifically on her reluctance to talk to, and walk away from, her partner. She is much stronger now, opening up physically and able to face the transition she will have to make' (Clayton, personal communication).

A difficult balancing act

Every practitioner knows that the patient has walked into the consulting room with the hope they will be made to feel better. In the following forty-five minutes, the practitioner in turn hopes to achieve that objective while at the same time assessing, and listening, perhaps psychologically nudging forward stuck material. The practitioner knows that they are required to prove to the patient that their particular healing discipline works – the reason, after all, for that consultation. They are also required to ask open questions, the better to heal; to be cautious not to tread into inappropriate territory, as we have already seen; to be penetrating enough harmlessly to stir, unblock or release. All this within the parameters of healing, restoring the fragmentation of the whole, and yet doing so with the minimum of invasion: of the patient's stacked up psycho-emotional agenda; of the time allocation for hands-on treatment; of their own personal needs. It is a balancing act of gigantic proportion.

Even the best, most experienced practitioners can get it wrong. Those with impeccable training credentials, a long history of personal therapy ensuring their personal material does not get in the way of their clients' own process, and with a wide patient base, can falter. The writer knows of a homeopath who got caught in negative transference with two of his clients. In his concern to keep the professional relationship boundaried, he refused to laugh at the first patient's defensive jokes where a beginner might well have chuckled appreciatively *and* prescribed the same remedy. The second patient found herself reporting untruthfully to him on the telephone ring-back appointment that her health had improved as a result of the homeopathic treatment suggested, aware only that she wanted to please the practitioner, not fail at being 'a good patient, like a good girl for Daddy'. Because childhood fears are often present in this type of intimate, one-to-one situation, the danger of such transference should never be underestimated. In this case, despite the integrity and perceptiveness of the homeopath concerned, they proved unhelpful for the therapeutic alliance and both patients left prematurely.

The significance of trust

To transfer distrust from childhood on to the practitioner can clearly impede the healing potential. The homeopath referred to above was unconsciously viewed by the first patient as a headmaster, summoning her to his study. But if pleasing the grown-up in authority is not the issue, then some other form of distrust may seep into the patient–practitioner relationship. For example, one acupuncture patient was adversely affecting the course of her treatment by her negative approach to its perceived invasion. Needles piercing the skin are, of course, a form of invasion but usually not a problem for patients, when they understand the balancing of chi energy and the consequent healing that results from it. Yet this particular patient was sabotaging her own treatment. She reported: 'I came to realize I was saying "Keep out!" to needles in just the same way as my body had been saying to my boyfriend "keep out" sexually' (personal communication).

Fortunately, this was possible to resolve. Realizing that lack of trust went right back to the woman's childhood – echoed in the unsatisfactory current relationship with the boyfriend – the practitioner had the opportunity to handle treatment in stages. Because her patient articulated her fears about invasion, the acupuncturist could enter into dialogue with her and suggest a programme wherein the patient decided when she was ready to advance, to risk penetration. The pain of childhood, where she had been the unconscious burden-bearer for her entire family's fearfulness, would be transcended somewhat now that the acupuncturist could be seen as a type of Good Mother, neither blaming nor cajoling.

Earning trust, as we have seen, can be a complex business particularly when hidden agendas (such as the 'headmaster's study' above) interfere in ways few practitioners could be expected to predict and manage to work round. As we have also seen, if there is the chance to talk about a patient's fears, creative ways forward might be forged. But in an initial session, it is not always easy to detect the dynamics in the room, above and beyond early impressions of transference and counter-transference. Many patients are diffident, shy, possibly embarrassed. How does the practitioner decide there are major childhood terrors lurking, which will continue to whisper menacingly unless the patient flees the relationship? As Jane Robinson points out, the face a patient presents in the consulting room can be very different from the one presented to the outside world. 'Sometimes I see someone sitting in the [crowded] waiting room, sad and down-trodden. They smile when they finally meet me, and I have to remember what I saw first, when they didn't realize who I was, and get back and find it because that was the truer reading' (personal communication).

If a practitioner works from home without a waiting room, they may not have the advantage of catching sight of any tell-tale body language before the one-to-one meeting. Psychological armoury (Lowen 1958: 134) may certainly be apparent – tightly closed knees, arms folded across the chest, a reluctance to make eye contact – yet these signs are not clear enough indications in themselves that the patient is frightened. Wary, yes, or possibly depressed; but the underlying cause for ultimately running away from treatment could be locked away in the psyche only to surface in, say, long-term psychotherapy. No holistic practitioner can be expected to do that level of excavation work.

Some prospective patients present with jolly laughter, interested questioning, arms and legs loose, for all the world paying a social call; and yet, hidden from view, anxiety thuds and the child–parent dynamic has already started. This might be an opportunity for the practitioner to delve a little deeper, perhaps by asking something like: 'How do you feel about that . . .?', or, 'It must be hard for you, having to . . .', thereby treading gently into the territory that is frightening the patient, and providing an open door for their tentative responses. However, it may prove difficult to pursue and this might suggest postponement until another session.

In a later chapter, we look further at developing this kind of dialogue. For the present, it is important issues about trust within the patient–practitioner alliance that need our more immediate attention. Issues of trust come in many guises, covering aspects that are not always understood or respected by alternative therapists. Within its various training programmes mainstream practice in the holistic field has disciplines and instructions designed to safeguard the profession as a whole and patients and practitioners in particular. Unfortunately, there are lesser known therapies (widely used nonetheless) whose training bodies do not yet monitor ongoing professional conduct, or teach the value of the disciplines adhered to by mainstream complementary practice. According to Edzard Ernst (quoted in Naish 2004: 7), there is still no regulation at all with many of these therapies 'that have substantial potential for doing harm'. Although mainstream practitioners are answerable to their training organizations, it is a fact that at the beginning of the present century only two – osteopathy and chiropractic – were regulated by government safeguards to ensure their qualification to practise. Currently, anyone can set up as a therapist in any other alternative field, with or without professionally rigorous training: a troubling state of affairs little recognized, apparently. *The Times* conducted a survey at the end of 2003 and discovered that many people mistakenly believe standards and training in complementary therapies are tightly regulated. They are not. This leaves the door wide open for patient abuse, of course, and a plethora of other difficulties both medical and psychological.

One obvious example of abuse is sexual contact between practitioner and patient. Are we completely sure the 'no sex' rule is respected throughout the alternative healing community? Violation of trust in this particular context is of the worst kind, betrayal at its most destructive, because a patient is at her or his most vulnerable. In therapeutic terms, even a love affair gently evolving from an encounter in the consulting room is problematical. Consider an extension of the child–parent transference, now energized by sexual contact: we can guess that it will end in tears because the dynamic continues in this unequal partnership, even where the treatment has finished. The damage is all the more intense precisely because the boundaries of the consultancy have been transgressed. If the 'parent' abandons the 'child' at some future point (no doubt weary of the dependence and wanting instead a peer relationship), the pain of separation is all the greater for the ex-patient, because they then experience a double betrayal. Conversely, the break-up might be created by the 'child', still caught unconsciously in unresolved issues with their real parent and needing to punish, or run away from recreated hurt. Mental health professionals know that unfinished business emotionally can haunt many a marital partnership, and that problems decades old can interfere with current new relationships (Skynner and Cleese 1983: 49). They also know that this is work for long-term therapy, certainly not material for lovers to try to disentangle.

Boundaries exist for good reasons

So crucial are the firm 'lines' in holding the therapeutic alliance – what we call boundaries – that some branches of the healing professions, such as psychotherapy and counselling, make it a fundamental rule there should be no fraternizing outside the therapy room, little or no personal disclosure on the part of the therapist within the consulting room, and no pleasantries exchanged such as the borrowing of books, objects taken away which have belonged to the therapist, and no introductions made to benefit either person. Is this overzealous? Probably not: it is a sensible safeguard to protect the 'blank screen' effect required in psychotherapy whereby the client can see themself reflected, as if looking in a mirror. As Mitchell and Cormack (1998: 118) point out:

> If enough care is taken to create clear boundaries, then the therapeutic relationship may become a safe place where the patient can feel relieved of the expectations which pertain in the ordinary encounters elsewhere in his life. He can then become free to try out new ways of being and relating which may be more productive and which may facilitate the changes he needs to make. This is why friendship (social meeting outside the therapeutic context) may impede the change possibilities created by the therapeutic relationship.

Of course, rules can be broken – or, rather, careful consideration might be given to bending a rule, as experienced practitioners sometimes do, fully conscious of what it is they seek to achieve. But first, the rules need to be learned and obeyed for a long time. Novice complementary practitioners do not usually have the personal psychological development necessary to afford considering taking risks. They are unaware of the dangers they run in blurring boundaries, or in breaking the psychological holding so necessary to the healing situation. It is essential that practitioners first familiarize themselves with the concept and value of boundaries.

Confidentiality is another important aspect of trust. If a patient should hear her practitioner speak about another patient (however anonymously), it creates unease at the least, instant alarm at worst. Their thinking may run along these lines: 'If he mentions so and so, even without naming them but describing a fair bit about them so that they could be identifiable, then what about me? Would he talk about *me*?' Practitioners might offer information without realizing the damage they could be causing, unaware that in mentioning other people, their personal stories, or even light gossip, they have broken confidence. Confidentiality in the consulting room must be the rule. No practitioner should feel free to talk about any patient, past, present or future, or they run the risk of losing their immediate patient's trust. There are professional codes of conduct outlined for mainstream complementary disciplines. Unfortunately, not all alternative therapies have such codes, and until there is a unilateral policy of accreditation (and therefore monitoring) throughout the alternative field, we must accept that poor quality practice does exist in the context of a need for firmly structured working frameworks.

The opening session

A practitioner's first responsibility is to create – and keep – an atmosphere of safety, reliability and trustworthiness (all good parenting), one therefore vital from the very first session. Skilled therapists know how important that initial meeting is. Jane Robinson again: 'The first few *seconds* are vital. I learn more about a patient in those moments than really at any other time – how they shake hands, make or fail to make eye contact, take their seat and so on. I try to match their pace and realize every moment is a testing situation. Cracking a joke can be good, or it can meet with a dull thud in those early moments of getting to know one another. If it's a dull thud, I ask myself was it me, or are they quite unable to open up? I work on a softly, softly approach, watching and waiting to see what's going on, treating only what I have observed, and that is all. For example, a patient's pulse could offer further clues about her distressed state and I might ask, "Is there something bugging you?", without moving in any further. If that produces a strong denial, I most certainly would not argue my findings suggest otherwise. But in the next session, it might be that she tells me she went home and started kicking doors down – and then we have the start of a trusting relationship' (personal communication).

Some patients expect alternative medicine to help them gain insight into what is wrong with their lives, already half guessing that the presenting physical complaint may only be the acceptable tip of an otherwise frightening and incomprehensible iceberg of difficulties. Millenson (1995: 133) says: 'Since part of the job of the holistic practitioner is to help the patient find "the healer within", there will often be times when it is impossible to separate the practice of complementary medicine from something very like psychotherapy.' As Capra (1988: 201) notes on the work of oncologist Carl Simonton, we can be of great value merely by learning to listen, by assuring our patients that negative feelings of anger, anxiety or depression are very natural ones, appropriate to the situation in which they find themselves, and not something to be hidden or suppressed out of shame.

Thus we already see that listening empathically, noting carefully the presenting physical symptoms as well as the first impressions of the person behind those symptoms – how they speak, look, sit – are important initial steps in the healing process. For a patient simply to be able to talk to somebody about their problems, where prescriptive advice-giving is never an option, can be enormously therapeutic. Millenson again:

> To the degree we can manage to be open, accepting and genuine human beings ourselves, and not hide behind professional roles, we can model the kinds of attributes that psychotherapeutic research has found create positive changes in clients' self-esteem, increase their ability to handle potential stressors, induce greater flexibility in the face of unpredictable life events, and lead clients to greater acceptance of themselves. It is the very acceptance and integration of our own life experience, the congruence between our own feelings and behaviour, and our own self-esteem – in short, our own being – rather than any set of techniques, that proves the most valuable asset in assisting patients with their problems of living.
>
> (1995: 133)

The idea of the Wounded Healer, one who has been forged by suffering in their own life, is central to most disciplines. Studies of the childhood and family life of therapists (Henry 1966; Burton 1970; Spurling and Dryden 1989, as cited by McLeod 1998: 354) have found a number of factors which appear to be related to later career choice. Therapists (and we may include complementary practitioners here) have often as children experienced loneliness, illness, bereavement or the need to look after others, from an early age. Brightman (1984: 295) has said: 'The role of therapist itself may constitute a re-enactment of an earlier situation in which a particularly sensitive and empathic child has been pressed into the service of understanding and caring for a parent (usually a depressed mother) figure.' As McLeod (1998: 354) points out, the child in this situation grows up with a need to care for others. The presence of such a 'wound' in a healer gives them an excellent basis from which to understand and empathize with the wounds of clients. But, McLeod adds: 'A danger is that the wound of the healer is exacerbated by the demands of those being helped, and the healer is sacrificed for their benefit . . . To be "good enough" to help people who are deeply damaged by life is to make a strong statement about one's own sanity, knowledge and competence' (1998: 355).

Once more we see the need for personal therapy as a background support to professional training in complementary therapies (or following training, though this is not as preferable). The mental health and stability of a practitioner is of paramount importance, just as it is for their supervisors and trainers, since no one is free of the psychic – or psychological – impact of others' 'baggage' and the consequent interaction, however unseen or unrecognized that might be.

Summary

Not all patients want, or expect, counselling when they come for treatment, although many already will have some awareness that their illness and emotional distress are linked. Pushing an unwilling, resistant newcomer may well prove counterproductive, though covert open questioning might offer important clues to help the treatment forward. Penetrating a situation, weighing up what is best now for the patient while at the same time assessing the treatment programme they need, is a difficult balancing act. Building up trust and creating a safe environment in which a vulnerable patient feels secure and unthreatened are both essential aspects of good practice. Furthermore, the therapeutic alliance needs firm boundaries. This is an absolute requirement and should always be respected: it creates a safe place where the patient can lower their defences without fear of invasion or abuse, and so permit the healing work to proceed more smoothly.

In the next chapter, we look at the subtle but crucial difference between ordinary conversational skills and professional listening, and examine how we need to be alert to other levels of communication.

Chapter **3**

How to listen through the words

There are differences between ordinary, passive and active listening, or, to put it another way, between engaging in a conversation and in working professionally. As we have already seen, an empathic and caring interest in which we show the other person that they have our attention, is potentially healing and a step towards the counselling process. But empathy is not enough; nor is caring deeply enough. What we are aiming for in using counselling skills is an *active* participation in moving things forward, in ways that are more than enabling the patient to feel heard.

As Rowan (1983: 30) points out: 'Why listening is so difficult to the new therapist is because there is a lot of unlearning to be done. In most conversations, we are formulating a reply when the other person is talking, so as to be ready when he or she finishes; we are going back and forth between what is being said and our reply, so that we never really hear properly all that is said.' All therapists, whether of the talking treatment kind, or complementary practitioners whose primary training is their particular healing field, should nonetheless remember that they need to be alert to other levels of communication.

Active listening involves exploring the meaning behind some statements. For example, a patient might come in and say, 'That traffic warden outside really pisses me off!' To which, if you were a friend, you might well reply, 'Oh, I know, they're awful –

one caught me last week and I think I may have to pay a fine and I'm feeling really angry . . .' But that, in the therapeutic role, would be to miss the point. Why is this patient leading off the entire session with an expletive about an unknown traffic warden? What is the real content of this outburst? Could it be anger much closer to home, such as anger with the practitioner (remember, he or she is unconsciously representing authority, parent or teacher), or maybe with their husband or wife? The patient might have decided not to talk in the treatment room about their marriage troubles and had instead vented their bottled up rage by projecting it elsewhere – in this case blaming the warden for *his* uncaring behaviour.

Alternatively, if the problem lies in disappointment with the treatment so far, then they dare not be direct with the practitioner for fear of reprisal of some sort, along similar lines to the homeopath's client who had to keep up her Daddy's Good Girl image (page 16). So, whatever the agenda, hidden or otherwise, we need to realize an unexpected expletive may quite possibly mean something other than the obvious. The practitioner, instead of replying casually, needs mentally to query the true butt of that anger. This might mean reflecting back: 'You seem very upset today. Perhaps it's not only the warden you feel pissed off about,' in the hope that the response will elicit more information. This response could be described as active listening, and, for the purpose of counselling in complementary practice, is a particularly useful professional tool.

Passive listening has its place

Provided there is good eye contact, an occasional nod of understanding and a smattering of minimal responses ('Ah-ha! Uh-hum!') wherever appropriate, passive listening can be helpful for the voluble patient who simply wants to offload before treatment can begin. In general terms, a patient can often bring their own thought-out solution to their immediate problem with little or no intervention from the therapist. If they are used to expressing their feelings, are comfortable about revealing their private lives and know that the practitioner needs to hear an authentic summary of today's 'top story', then a new scenario could run like this: 'I'm feeling really angry today, especially after a row with that traffic warden outside. But it's reminding me of the fury I've been carrying about my husband. We had a bad quarrel a few days ago and I thought John was being totally unfair. And yet it was over such a trivial thing, really, a silly mix up . . . I feel better now I've told you. Perhaps I'll call John from my mobile later and apologize for my side of the misunderstanding.'

Passive listening does not mean remaining silent. It can be supplemented by various neutral, invitational openers such as, 'Would you like to say some more about it?', or 'I'd be interested to hear how you feel about that.' Another form of passive listening is, as it were, hearing what the body has to 'say', something complementary practitioners are already familiar with. Posture, defensive crossing of arms and legs and other gestures are all significant bearers of messages so that even if the patient withholds part of their 'top story', their body will probably communicate additional material to help us gain a fuller picture. Breathing, too, can be revealing – its rate and depth. Secretly copying that rate can sometimes help to inform the practitioner of how their patient is feeling.

Of course, a healer does not necessarily need to know the minutiae of their patient's quarrel, whereas some counsellors or psychotherapists might consider such knowledge important. What should concern the practitioner is being able to move forward in their treatment, taking into account the strong emotional content present and having some understanding of the underlying causes, which could be throwing up other areas needing their attention.

'Valuable as passive listening and door openers are for opening up communication lines,' Millenson reflects (1995: 135), 'there is another kind of special listening that therapists do which is far more active; it is a skill that counsellors generally have to work at to acquire. This kind of listening is known as active or empathic listening, the importance of which for helping relationships was first emphasized by the distinguished humanistic psychologist Carl Rogers.' Millenson states that in active listening the therapist is listening not just *to* the words, but also *through* the words for the feeling tone or emotion that lies behind them. Once having picked up that feeling tone the therapist will feed it back to the speaker. Millenson goes on:

How does this work? First of all, since it's impossible to get inside another's skin, note that no one, not even the most sensitive and skilled friend, lover or counsellor, ever knows exactly what another person is experiencing. However, by listening closely to what is heard and how it is said, as well as attending closely to gestures and other non-verbal signals . . . one is able to make plausible inferences about another's feelings. Consider for a moment the patient as a sender in a communication receiver. He has an experience or a feeling that he wishes to share with you, so he has first to select the appropriate words, which constitutes a code that will represent these inner feelings. On hearing those words, you – the receiver – have to decode them to guess or infer the sender's experience.

(1995: 136)

Active listening is far more than a skill used to ensure that speaker and listener communicate effectively: it fosters two of the most important ingredients for a healthy human relationship. Those ingredients are *empathy* and *acceptance*. Yet why do we need to learn these fundamental interpersonal skills? Why are these apparently valuable resources, so useful to all forms of contact, not natural phenomena which appear alongside the wish to help or, indeed, to get on better with others? The answer is manifold. We could point to social and cultural differences; we could blame our general lack of emotional literacy, recalling that one generation at least was encouraged to be seen and not heard (how stultifying for children, in their natural zest to tell it how it really is); and we could also reflect upon the British people being encouraged, throughout the experiences of two world wars, to play down bad experience. Consider the stiff upper lip heroes, never given to hyperbole, who shrugged off pilot fatality with a terse, 'Johnson "bought it", I'm afraid; jolly poor show'; and, in the current business jargon 'We're going to have to let you go . . .', to an unsuspecting employee. In neither case does the speaker actually tell it how it really is and we are left to grapple with euphemism.

As we saw earlier, it is our instinctive reaction on hearing bad news to express sympathy, to ask concerned amplifying questions, or to move on to cap the story with a personal anecdote as a way of showing we understand and appreciate what the other person is trying to tell us. But this seldom works in the counselling environment, beyond an initial – and brief – show of genuine emotional response. The way must be clear for the patient to feel free to continue; and, of course, the same is true should the material be joyful, good news. This will seem strange to those who have not yet learned listening skills and who have so far conversed through listening and responding as they might in a social situation.

What goes wrong with ordinary listening

Even when we manage to decipher this other meaning, we are not necessarily left with a clear sense of how the person actually feels about what they have said. All practitioners will have heard their patients reply to the opening well-being query with, 'Fine', 'OK', or 'Not too bad', knowing they will have to wait for a real sense of the position. For example, they might need to repeat the phrase used, with a question mark in their voice so that the patient is encouraged to expand on it. If we look again at the first mode in listening mentioned at the start of this chapter – what Rowan (1983: 31) calls ordinary listening – we might begin to see why it can put a block on the kind of communication needed in the therapeutic alliance. Remember, as Rowan says, in ordinary listening we are trying to relate the other person's experience to our own and we are thinking of interesting replies to carry on the conversation and keep 'our end up'. Holding the superior position like this (however unintentional) effectively halts any further exploration.

As to other ways of inhibiting useful exploration, Millenson cites no fewer than twelve *communication roadblocks*, which generally, and destructively in therapeutic terms, communicate our desire to influence or change the other person in the way that we think appropriate:

> These responses usually come from our own need to get the other person to change their way of thinking, feeling or behaving to conform to what we believe is appropriate. Sometimes we give such responses because we are

uncomfortable with their feelings. Because these typical automatic responses (1) inhibit the person from getting in touch with deeper feelings, (2) retard their natural problem solving ability, and (3) often engender resentment and anger directed back at the listener for trying to control them, these responses are appropriately called roadblocks to communication . . . They are also roadblocks to creating the kind of patient–practitioner relationship that will both create a healing climate and optimise the patient's adherence to whatever treatment plan evolves. So it is vital to recognise and avoid them wherever possible.

(1995: 137)

When a practitioner intentionally moves from a problem-solving, solution-oriented mode into 'counselling mode' she must be wary about sending a message of non-acceptance. For each of the roadblocks conveys the listener's intent to *change*, rather than *accept*, the speaker. Such a climate of non-acceptance is not conducive to personal growth, development and emotional health because, as Millenson points out, when people feel judged, analysed or put down, they become defensive, closed and resistant to change. 'This is not a mood conducive to healing, and if the patient generates stress responses to her practitioner's non-acceptance of her feelings, physical problems can definitely be exacerbated' (Millenson 1995: 140).

Practitioners do need to ask questions

No practitioner can do the job they were trained for without asking questions of the patient, not only of the open door variety but leading, forthright requests for information. Obviously, this can be a difficult area in itself – older patients, for example, might be uncomfortable about talking about sexual matters, or their bowel motions – and sensitive emotional holding of these awkward moments is a required part of the healing meeting. The more intimate the details, often the more useful they are for the practitioner. But how to collect those details without being experienced as intrusive, prurient or anything else objectionable to the patient? As Ned Reiter warns:

It's always a good idea to check 'Do I need to go down that route?' if a patient reports their life is fine and all the signals I pick up are that they are not fine. Challenging is seldom a good idea (I rarely confront) but I might casually say 'You mentioned a few weeks back that there was a lot going on in your life. Is there much stress around for you now?' If I have noticed bruising and guess marital problems, that type of question is a good one to bring out the cause of the pain.

We are often the first contact patients make in getting help. They might feel an inability to share their secret with friends, neighbours or their GP and not ready to book an appointment to see a counsellor or psychotherapist. It's more socially acceptable to be seen to visit a herbalist. Complementary practitioners tend to get the first 'spilling out' and it's important to let them off-load without my jumping in with cues and stirring things up, because I cannot send them out gibbering, with head and heart ripped open. It is important for a practitioner not to step outside his area of expertise. Using counselling skills in my work tells me what I *can* do and those skills prevent me doing what I *cannot* do. What I give is medicine to support them in their stress, and compassion in listening to their story. If it is a big one – such as wife battering, or their son is a heroin addict – I encourage them anyway to come back to me. If that first off-loading felt right for the patient, they will return a couple more times for further medicine and then that might be the right session to suggest they seem readier to talk to an expert about their domestic problems.

(personal communication)

But what if the patient does not choose to take their problems elsewhere? This poses a new set of questions for the practitioner. In general terms (and, again, always remembering the Good Parent transference), patients might well feel so comfortable with the regularity of their appointments that they are reluctant to stop making them. Assuming there are no momentous reasons for a referral to psychotherapy, the practitioner recognizes these appointments might continue because the patient simply enjoys talking. Their visits suggest dependence and the practitioner must address that dependence.

These, then, are the types of questions the practitioner will need to ask themself: 'Am I encouraging this? Am I colluding with this person? Am I doing harm by agreeing to keep seeing them?' Clear-sighted inner reflection is necessary. Personal awareness (learned best as a client in therapy) can be helpful in discovering the answers. Collusion can seldom be therapeutic, largely because collusion suggests an intertwining of personal needs, an unhealthy co-dependence. Yet there will be times when an experienced alternative healer does permit this, conscious of the dangers but mindful too of the value derived by the patient in having a comforting haven from which to escape temporarily a stressful, or lonely, life.

One Reike Master reports that she considers part of her heal-ing practice includes a decision to encourage one particular patient to talk non-stop for half an hour before she is ready to climb on to the bed for her treatment. It is as if 'letting off steam' and regularly updating her practitioner is a necessary prelude for the patient to benefit most from this ancient Tibetan healing method. Such an example offers a useful learning point, however. As Thelma Buckley said: 'If counselling skills had been part of my two-year Reike training preparation, I believe I would have been much more use to my patient than merely sympathetically listen-ing to her thirty minute monologue each time' (personal communication).

Another practitioner points to the difficulty she experienced when she once tackled her long-term patient with: 'I feel you are still coming here because we have fallen into a quasi-counselling situation and it is time you went to see a real counsellor.' She sensed immediately that the patient felt this to be a hurtful put down. Several practitioners I interviewed voiced similar observa-tions about this general dilemma, adding such comments as: 'If I am aware I have not encouraged the dependency, then perhaps it is acceptable to continue to listen to them, as long as they clearly need it.'

Asking questions requires a gentle, open-ended and thera-peutic approach. If it is too abrupt and disjointed, such as when a practitioner clearly has other things on his mind (distracted by a ringing telephone, say, or an ambulance noisily speeding by), a sudden intervention can jar the patient. The likelihood is they will either freeze on their memories or feel disinclined to launch into revealing anything or that the thoughtless intervention effectively becomes another roadblock.

We might bear in mind here that people with emotional problems have been involved in relationships in which their experience was denied, defined or discounted by others. McLeod (1998: 97) suggests: 'What is healing is to be in a [therapeutic] relationship in which the self is fully accepted and valued. Of course, some people are so locked into a self-evaluation defined from being ignored in childhood they will have developed a defense against that pain.' Dryden and Feltham (1992) highlight the need to be sensitive to the nuances involved when people talk effusively but aimlessly, perhaps out of embarrassment or avoidance.

> How do you allow clients to talk, as we suggest, while at the same time deciding when talk is cathartic and useful, or defensive or rambling? In the case of someone who is genuinely and acutely distressed you will instinctively listen without a need to intervene. In the case of someone who is trying with difficulty to disclose significant information, your ability to respond empathically is a key skill, but you will also need to initiate some subtle structuring.
>
> (Dryden and Feltham 1992: 43)

Reining in the over-talkative

Complementary practitioners have limited time to counsel their patients. The time they feel appropriate to give to this aspect of the work will depend on the nature of the healing discipline perhaps, and certainly on each new occasion as it arises. At one point it may feel essential to let the patient talk themselves out; at another, a false economy of allocation for active listening, when the emphasis of the session must lie elsewhere. As we have already seen, juggling various needs in any one consultation can be professionally demanding and an extremely difficult balancing act.

There is a call, then, for some structure, albeit a loose one, should the healer decide on the spur of the moment that their patient's paramount need is to pour out her emotional issues. Usually, practitioners learn to divide their time in such a way as to give one hundred per cent listening attention to the opening stages (where so much information is gleaned to help the treatment forward), and offering interventions to encourage that stage along. Then they get down to the 'hands-on' healing, whatever form that might take. At this point, while continuing to use their listening skills and remaining alert to any other important clues emerging, they are unlikely to forget it is their primary holistic goal to send the patient away feeling better. This might be the moment to rein in the over-talkative patient. As Dryden and Feltham (1992: 45) point out: 'She may ramble on indefinitely. If you allow her to, she may well waste her time and money. She may also get quite the wrong impression of counselling and *need* to have someone help her focus. This kind of interrupting isn't rudeness and it isn't against the rules of counselling!'

But how to rein in the runaway rambler? It might be helpful to say gently: 'I am a little unclear about why you are telling me about your sister's guinea pig. Could you explain to me how this may be affecting your feelings?' Or, 'I need to check out with you to make sure I've understood this correctly – has talking about your sister brought up feelings you want to explore? Sometimes a family incident can bring back all sorts of unexpected memories and I'm wondering if you would like to say some more about that?' Probably this will prove to be a non-starter, but at least the voluble speaker can be harmlessly shepherded into more therapeutic territory.

Summary

There are three different kinds of listening. The first is ordinary, everyday conversation; the other two are a more professional type of listening called passive and active, carrying the express purpose of hearing *through* the words used, so formulating a better sense of the feeling tone or emotion lying behind them. Ordinary listening has the dangerous potential to block communication and implies a wish to influence or change the other person. This approach should not be used in the therapy room: it can close down the patient's urge to say more, and the climate of non-acceptance may even make them angry and defensive, perhaps to the point of exacerbating their physical symptoms.

Practitioners may need to halt an over-talkative patient when loquaciousness is a cover-up for avoidance of looking at more painful feelings. These, of course, could well lie at the root of their somatic distress. Over-talkativeness, florid or extravagant phrases and gestures can all provide the practitioner with important additional clues as to what their patient might really be feeling. In the following chapter, we look further at learning to recognize these unconscious 'hidden messages'.

Chapter 4

Metaphors and mind magic

When people describe their physical symptoms or state of mind, they often feel the need to explain them to the therapist in 'as if' terms. They use metaphor as a means of communicating the nearest possible way to tell their truth. How many times do we hear snippets in everyday conversation that underline this? Comments like, 'That man is a pain in the backside . . . I shall explode if he walks all over me again at the meeting.' We know that none of this is literally true, and yet we get a clear idea of the grievance the speaker wants to convey.

If this is useful in conversation, then consider how much more so it might be in the consulting room. When a patient presents to the osteopath with a painful lower lumbar region that reveals (after exhaustive tests) no obvious physiological cause, the practitioner might wonder what is going on in the patient's life that might offer a clue to the cause of the discomfort. This is where counselling techniques can help. 'You seem quite tense in that area – I'm wondering if there's much stress going on for you at the moment?' The patient could well respond immediately to this open question, grateful to have found a listening ear and ready to speak, for example, of difficulties at home with her grown-up son. The osteopath will probably have already guessed at anger as the root cause of her physical discomfort, but the fact that his patient is starting to express some of it will facilitate healing.

So he might encourage the narrative with empathy and active listening, reflecting back to the patient what she might be experiencing: 'I wonder if you feel it's high time your son left home, but you are holding yourself back from actually pushing him out because as a loving mother you don't want to do it that way. This sounds difficult for you: it seems you find yourself caught between two strong feelings . . .' This probably sums up the inner conflict this mother finds herself in. Her lower back is somatizing that conflict, tensing the very muscles her angry self wants to employ to do the 'pushing'.

Clearly, this understanding can be further explored and perhaps practitioner and patient can together release some of her blocked up emotions, freeing the mother to see better what tension has done to her body (the need to get something or somebody off her back) and to allow more space for choice. This may mean she can *consciously* elect now, if relief is still not possible, to accept her back pain for as long as it takes to wait for her son's voluntary departure; or she could open up discussion at home to tell him of her needs and to negotiate a 'nest-leaving' date. Either way, the osteopath's interventions will have been valuable.

Backing out of conflict

Another typical context for psychosomatic back pain occurs in the employment field. Workers unconsciously want to back out of a boring job; or back out of taking on more, yet unrewarding, responsibility at work. When emotions are involved in a major way, holistic practitioners can usually assume there is inner conflict at the root of physical discomfort. Backs also 'go out' when guilty conscience prods: let's say an illicit affair beckons and one party struggles with their need for passion on the one hand and their fear of wrongdoing on the other. This conflict can result in dramatic, eleventh-hour physical collapse, where the stress causes actual physiological trauma, thus ensuring a plausible reason for 'backing out' of attending the lovers' tryst and going instead to the chiropractor; yet the patient has no idea what has caused this disappointing outcome and will sincerely point to an external event – lifting, stretching, bending, perhaps – which has accidentally sabotaged the longed-for union. As Shilling (1993: 3) writes: 'We now have the means to exert an unprecedented degree of control over bodies, yet we are also living in an age which has thrown into radical doubt our knowledge of what bodies are and how we should control them.'

The difficulty most of us face in learning how to control our bodies lies firstly in realizing how our emotional issues manifest in physical symptoms. At a simplistic level we can, of course, recognize a particular person gives us a pain in the neck, as we ruefully register the taut muscles and aching head likely to follow. But, as we have noticed from the above, a mother deep in conflict about her son leaving home may not recognize the significance of her painful back and it might take 'talking treatment' as well as osteopathy to help her unravel the body's message. As Totton (2003: 77) notes: 'Working with repressed experience on the bodily level allows for very precise focus, and can sidestep some forms of psychological avoidance . . . Once we actually become aware "from the inside" of how we are holding on with the muscle, we automatically become able to relax it and the experience which we are holding back automatically enters our awareness.'

The body can give messages in many astonishing ways. Take Sally's story, which begins when she presented with a problem in swallowing. A young woman, she was diagnosed by a hospital consultant as having a condition called globus hystericus, a nervous disorder which in effect stopped her taking in nourishment. As a child, Sally had experienced a loveless family life in which her parents' dogmatic religious views were constantly discussed.

> My parents' beliefs were thrust down my throat and I hated it. When I grew up I had low self-esteem, felt very unworthy and increasingly uneasy about eating certain 'chewy' foods. Eventually, I couldn't swallow much and grew thinner and thinner. So I went to a homeopath to get help for my emotional state, once I had clearance from the hospital that there was nothing organically wrong.
>
> My homeopath, who had trained in counselling, was really helpful. She asked about my childhood and soon spotted the tie up with my not wanting to 'ingest' the dogma. Then, after a few sessions talking around all of this, including my panic attacks and depression, she pointed out I didn't seem to be enjoying life at all. She gently added that it

was no wonder an unconscious part of me was reluctant to take in food – it equated with the childhood dogma and with my suicidal feelings. Basically, if I didn't eat I would conveniently die and then all my sadness and lovelessness would be over. Once I realized what that child aspect in me was unconsciously directing me to do, and that I could choose my own views and opinions now, I felt a different person! Eating hasn't been a problem since and I am quite clear about wanting to nourish rather than starve myself.

(personal communication)

Body cells remember

Another patient recalls humiliating times in her bullied childhood when she was told roughly to 'Hold your tongue!' and 'That's quite enough of your lip . . . ' only to discover in her fifties that she had contracted cancer of her tongue and her lip. Coincidence? Of course it could be: but the patient herself is convinced there is a connection with those earlier emotional traumas. She began to realize the parts of her body that figured in times of her worst despair somehow became the locus for her psychic burden to the point of dangerous vulnerability and predisposition to illness. Much the same could be said to apply in the case of a timorous middle-aged man, having to submit to a leg amputation after gangrene had set in following vascular problems. Unhappily married to a cold wife from whom he nonetheless felt reluctant to part, as it would mean riskily having to stand on his own two feet, his customary escape-from-pain credo had always been: 'Now I'll go to the pub, drown my sorrows and drink myself legless!' Another coincidence? Or does the mind lay down clues along the way for those who can spot them? One possible answer to this might lie with Carol Anthony (1988: 304) when she discusses the ego self-image:

The ego, here defined, is the composite of all the self-images we have ever adopted or would be tempted, through fantasy, to adopt. Once created, this composite self takes on a life of its own, and surrounds itself with a defensive and prideful barricade. It is as if we climb into a particular set of clothing because we like the way it looks, only to find that it dances off with us in it, out of control. It usurps leadership of the true self, and because it manifests itself as a pride system, it resists being displaced.

Anthony refers to our bodily and emotional impulses as 'inferiors', that is, when they are led by our ego they are in opposition to our true self. She adds: 'We find [the inferiors] are body cells, or systems of cells which seem to have a limited intelligence. This intelligence surfaces in our mind in such thoughts as "I am tired", or "I am hungry", or as other needs and wants. Like children, they usually respond willingly to suggestions, as when dentists or doctors give warning that "this will hurt only for a moment." If only we give them a bit of advance preparation, they will cooperate willingly.' Anthony goes on to say:

> Quick changes, for which they have little preparation, make them freeze with fear. Thus, when one small muscle in the back is strained, the surrounding cells freeze, *as if in fear they might be hurt next.* Often during our adult lives we simply repress them, living in our bodies as strangers. We may do any variety of things which stress them to their limits, such as going too many hours without sleep, failing to eat nutritious food, overworking, or drinking too much.
>
> (1988: 304, my italics)

Though this may not directly explain the correlation between childhood experience and disease much further down the line, we are faced nonetheless with an uncanny echo where specific parts of the body reflect the site of a psychological trauma, exemplified in the humiliated female patient with a cancerous tongue and lip and the fearful, legless man who had never felt empowered enough to risk autonomy. A connection between their 'defensive, prideful barricades' and their physical disabilities appears to exist, but until these areas generally are more fully researched, we must continue to point to the possibility of coincidence when these startling phenomena appear.

A further viewpoint, much in sympathy with Anthony, is introduced by Bloom (2001: 96), who says:

If your mental attitude to your body is detached, frigid, utilitarian, stoic, embarrassed, ashamed, resentful or harsh in any other way, this sends an ongoing signal of disapproval and alienation into the body. This in turn causes ongoing tension and perpetual anxiety. Your mind should give your body warmth, affection, encouragement, love, enthusiasm, care and extended authentic positive attention. This gets the endorphins flowing in abundance and releases all systems into an open flow.

For patients whose early emotional life lacked a model affirming these qualities, it is not difficult to see why the two people described earlier constructed a prideful, defensive barricade round themselves. A barricade means 'keep out', thus avoiding real contact, and ensuring the owner will stay safe from further painful invasion. Such was the belief of the child 'architect' of those protective screens when the surrounding dangers were pristine and therefore at their most threatening. I will demonstrate further examples of this, but first, a reminder about the importance of 'contact', an essential prerequisite for our health and well-being. Totton (2003: 76) suggests that the term is a metaphor derived from bodily experience, describing the state of being 'in touch' with oneself, with the world, or with another person.

> Contact is what makes the difference between touching one's lover or child and touching the person next to one on a commuter train. It is a condition of living relationship, which, as Gestalt therapy reminds us, depends on the ability to create a boundary between self and other: 'contact is the appreciation of differences'.
>
> (Fritz Perls, quoted in Heckler 1984: 119)

Armouring – or barricades – create a state of contactlessness. Totton (2003: 76) goes on to say that people may wear a mask of vitality and sociality, but be fundamentally out of touch with their own somatic and emotional experience, and similarly out of touch with others and the world around them.

Mind magic and imaginal clues

Counselling patients who can make links between the images their mind throws up and their illness is rewarding in itself and obviously contributes to their healing. If, on the other hand, a patient cannot accept the body's metaphor as an important part of understanding their sickness, then a practitioner may need to wait until chance offers a way forward. An eczema patient, for example, with ragingly irritating skin once asked for some herbal cream to relieve the itching. The medical herbalist treating her enquired about stresses in her life, leaving the counselling 'door' wide open, only to be told there were no stresses she could think of, absolutely not. Why, she had a lovely home, husband and children, garden, pets, job: her world, apparently, was a paradise on earth.

Then, suddenly: 'My mother-in-law is coming to stay soon. I know I shouldn't say it, but I really cannot stand her. She gets right under my skin with her bossiness but of course I'm powerless to stop her frequent visits because she is, after all, Alan's mother and our children's only grandma . . .' The patient was unaware of the pointed metaphor she had used, and of the clear message she had unintentionally given the practitioner; yet, as a result of her throwaway line, she received fuller herbal treatment because the medical herbalist could now address the hot rage in her system, in addition to the epidermal trouble. In time, she came to understand the parallel between her irritated resentment and the irritable skin condition; and ultimately, with the herbalist's encouragement, she found a new assertiveness to challenge some of her mother-in-law's controlling ways and relieve some of those trapped feelings.

A lowly self-image

Depressed people often have ways of describing themselves that use metaphors to powerful effect, because for them it is the most vivid way to convey how they feel. One of the most fascinating illustrations of this is to be found in the case of Anna, who announced one day to her therapist: 'I am a worm.' Formerly an overworked social worker, Anna had finally collapsed with a nervous breakdown. Her sense of self was severely dented by the collapse, yet her colleagues had no idea quite how poorly she had always viewed her worth.

Slowly her narrative unfolded: sexual abuse in childhood, abandoned by mother and farmed out to live with relatives. The sexually abused child, silent for fear of parental wrath about her 'dirty wickedness' with an uncle, had struggled into adult life and worked professionally as hard as she could to try to prove her worth, but had inevitably broken down when the job pressures intensified. Anna's metaphor, in trying to sum up her under-confident feelings that day, struck a useful note for the therapist. 'So you feel as if you are a worm. What comes into your mind if you say that word again?' Together, they explored Anna's mental associations (all pejorative), still without her recognizing the significance of the 'bad' worm adjectives she was offering. Unprompted, but electrifying in its impact, a memory erupted to the surface of her mind and in amazement she began talking about a long-forgotten childhood game.

Her cousin, a child with learning difficulties, had often wanted to play 'worm hospital': this entailed digging up worms, bandaging them and putting them in a pretend hospital ward. No children at their school would tolerate such strange play and the two girls were regularly 'sent to Coventry', neither spoken to nor their presence acknowledged in any way. At least for Anna there lay a distorted, but comforting, sense of togetherness in this isolation, a safe camaraderie with her eccentric cousin. She recognized as a client after her breakdown that both girls had acted out their respective needs to 'nurse the worm within', that unacceptable, disgusting part of themselves.

Anna's story emerged in psychotherapy, a different thera-peutic setting. The case is included here to highlight the significance of metaphor in the consulting room, a further example of the need for practitioners to pay close attention to their patients' choice of words at all times. Citing Angus and Rennie (1988), who were interested in the role of metaphor in therapy and who explored the issue of client or counsellor using novel or striking metaphor, McLeod (1998: 233) says: '[But] it is striking, when reading case studies published by counsellors and thera-pists, or listening to counsellors present cases at supervision, that very often the discussion of a case hinges on the meaning and significance of key moments or events.'

Being alert to whatever may emerge from the unconscious might seem like extra and unexpected responsibility for the hard-working complementary practitioner. It could, however, be a taste of things to come: for, as the government continues to tackle the lack of regulation nationwide, it is likely that more and more training bodies will enhance their curricula to include a working knowledge of psychodynamic concepts such as transference and counter-transference, projection and projective identification (these core concepts are described in Grant and Crawley (2002) and Rowan and Jacobs (2002)). Most reputable professional bodies already teach forms of listening skills, rapport-making and assessment of the patient's emotional state, under the heading of the dynamics of clinical practice, but counselling skills per se tend not to appear in any prospectus. The reason for this is unclear, though we could guess that if one professional discipline is increasingly to be melded to another (with the application of attendant criteria), the simplest way forward is to embrace them under new-sounding headings, such as patient-centred communication. However it is done, the movement is greatly to be celebrated and will, of course, serve patients better because it is not only more holistic but also more stringent.

Summary

Metaphor is a valuable tool in the complementary practitioner's kitbag. It can point to what patients are really feeling when they describe themselves in obviously inaccurate terms. Their unlikely choice of words can usefully convey the true picture, and we must remember to reflect carefully upon such apparent anomolies. Metaphors can say 'it's as if . . .' with imaginal precision in a way that straight narrative is unable to do: witness the speaker at the start of the chapter, who felt 'walked all over' by a disliked man. It is important also to pay careful attention to the shape of the images offered, as those shapes can speak of an emotional charge and act as a direct guide to the inner world of the patient, however much they might themselves be unaware of that inner world. The next chapter looks further at clinical settings in which practitioners can learn more about their patients' subtexts and how those hidden agendas can manifest in illness.

Chapter 5

The search for meaning in illness

Any discussion on the significance of metaphor in illness leads us almost inevitably to the question: is there any meaning in illness? Since the unconscious appears to try to convey messages via powerful imagery, or, as we saw in Chapter 4, through other nudges to jog the memory, could anything else lie behind these phenomena that practitioners could usefully heed? The link is an obvious one. But it is also seductive and might beckon us towards an oversimplistic, facile grasp of why people get sick.

When counselling, practitioners must be aware of the dangers inherent in reductionist diagnosis: 'Aha! This heart condition means a broken-hearted patient', or 'This woman with breast cancer must have issues around poor mothering', and so on. Those who espouse the holistic approach declare it *is* that simple, however. Louise Hay's *You Can Heal Your Life* (1984) is a classic publication underlying this approach, in which she suggests our thought patterns and the emotional states they evoke lead to some four hundred ailments. On the other hand, Jungian analysts Guggenbühl-Craig and Micklem regard the search for meaning in illness as futile and they criticize the pursuit as too judgemental:

> All these beautiful modern symbolic explanations are harmful in their very moralism. Sick people . . . not only have to suffer, but are made to feel guilty as well: their diseases are entirely their own fault; they have failed to develop

psychologically; they have suppressed their feelings or have not suppressed them enough; they have been too friendly, or not friendly enough.

(1988: 144)

Shealy and Myss (1988: 23) point out that symbolic analysis is not simple and it is certainly not obvious:

Understanding the emotional, psychological and spiritual stresses that underlie the creation of illness is a complex process. It is not like a game of connecting the dots in which eye problems connect to a desire not to see clearly, ear problems connect to a desire to tune something or someone out of a person's life, and leg problems signify difficulty in standing on one's own . . . People are complicated and their personal histories and emotional patterns are highly individual and complex.

Yet Freud's colleague, Georg Groddeck, who published a series of cases in the 1920s in his classic *The Meaning of Illness* (still widely quoted; 1977) mentions the case of a woman with generalized oedema resulting from congestive heart failure. The swollen tissues subsided immediately the woman had confessed to Dr Groddeck her guilt about marrying after she had made a vow to become a nun. Having broken her celibacy vow, she felt she deserved punishment, but found in her physician an acceptance which transcended the guilt. Subsequently she passed large quantities of urine and lost 50 pounds in one week. Groddeck's summary of the case was that the conflict between her heart and the guilt had created the disease. Once the conflict was resolved in sympathetic discussion – not unlike today's counselling – the condition improved dramatically.

The value of finding a meaning

Is there, then, meaning in illness, or is it multifactorial and therefore is the search for a subtext a spurious occupation? In looking for an answer, perhaps we should remember the value of paradox: both views might be true and it could prove helpful to allow for both, if only in the interest of ensuring an open, balanced approach. Millenson (1995: 211) suggests three reasons to look for meaning in a patient's illness:

> (1) Meaning is frequently valuable in the diagnosis and prognosis of a disease; (2) finding a meaning in an illness can prove to be an empowering source of hope and optimism for the patient; (3) interpretations in the form of possible life disharmonies suggest novel places to look for the causes of the illness, namely in how some fundamental physical, emotional or spiritual needs of the patient are not being fulfilled.

The value in asking ourselves questions about the symbolic meaning of disease or illness lies in the opportunity available to find out what is out of harmony in the patient. When a disease has been diagnosed, the use of medicine (in its widest sense), counselling, dietary changes and possibly lifestyle changes are all indicated to help the patient back, if possible, to some semblance of good health. Whether patients want to share this opportunity and discuss their illness with their practitioner is an individual matter: it must be realized that it is not everyone's wish (or belief system) to find a reason for their poor health – that may be to risk encountering uncomfortable issues – and the practitioner must take care not to impose his or her views of what the illness could mean. Mitchell and Cormack (1998: 69) point out: 'In treatment, if the patient and practitioner come to a shared understanding about the significance of the illness, then the practitioner can use the patient's perspective as a framework for her intervention in order to enable treatment to make more sense for the patient.' And Moss (1981: 105) comments:

> I no longer advocate transformation to everyone. I have realized that there is a natural inner timing and that people can be helped to go only as far as that allows. All judgement or coercion to go further must be released. It is natural for me now to accept and honour people as they are. People who are not ready cannot be brought forward into the fuller transformative energies even if it is clear that doing so could possibly release them from the forces configurating their illness.

Most complementary practitioners believe that work on the mind in holistic healing is axiomatic. But we operate in a multidimensional area and all is not quite as it might appear. We must not forget, for example, that one patient's asthma could be the result of childhood repetititive bronchitis; another's of having had to endure a suffocating, controlling mother; yet another's allergenic or stress induced – or maybe a bit of both. Each of us is unique in the configuration of predisposition, environmental factors and how we cope (or fail to cope) in our respective socio-cultural surroundings.

Thus, when a patient called Clare presented to her homeopath with irritable bowel syndrome (IBS), the practitioner took pains to delve deeply but carefully into her current and past medical history without a trace of significant psychological searching. She learned that Clare had been a talented freelance photographer who had finally had to give up work because IBS virtually disabled her. It was no use taking her camera out of doors: the daunting lack of lavatories close by made sorties into the countryside impossible.

Clare, a woman in her sixties, whose GP had been unable to find a cure, was defensive and strangely childlike as the mild questioning continued. She sat with arms folded in a protective gesture and gave silent 'Keep out!' facial signals. The practitioner experienced Clare as seething with suppressed rage, aware that her patient was figuratively 'sitting on a great deal of shit', but far too polite (socially) and cut off (psychologically) to be capable of owning her strong feelings.

After their first session, the homeopath prescribed a remedy which did offer some relief for the disturbed bowel condition. But on a later visit, the patient was clearly still locked in her rage, and not really improved. Clare happened to mention rummaging about in her attic the day before, looking through photos from a long-forgotten family album. Then she burst out: 'It was extraordinary! I just couldn't bring myself to look at a head-and-shoulders picture of my mother! Why on earth was that? I mean, Mother died 20 years ago!'

The homeopath moved in rapidly: 'You didn't want to look at your mother's face? What feelings come up for you as we consider that? . . . Oh, she always looked so disapprovingly at you, did she? That must have been very hurtful for you as a small child. I wonder if you can see the connection between that hurt and fear and your uncontrollable bowels?' Slowly, the significance of her mother still having enormous negative power dawned upon Clare, as she reflected upon the emotions that were visibly shaking her.

The practitioner felt it right now to encourage a few more revelations about Clare's over-controlled childhood. Suppressed anger was giving way fast to overtly expressed rage: the healing crisis had begun. It was only a matter of weeks before the IBS symptoms cleared up completely. However, with its departure Clare began to experience a painful depression: this was a clinically predictable sequence, now that the 'split off' part of her wounded childhood had been reintegrated into her conscious mind. The homeopath referred Clare on to psychotherapy, where she could explore her sadness more fully.

Being one step ahead

As we have seen, the unconscious mind releases messages in the form of imaginal or metaphorical clues and it also provides straight hints in the fact of a somatic symptom, such as a pain in the neck. This is where the practitioner yet once more needs to be one step ahead of their patient: not in jumping to conclusions based on a New Age 'we create our own reality' formula, but in guessing that there is psychological material *likely* to be connected significantly to the presenting problem and in need of encouraging to the surface.

Perhaps we should regard the symbolic Table of Disease, presented by countless holistic writers over the past two decades, simply as suggested guidelines: a new way of seeing illness and a supplement to other diagnostic systems. Take the amputee mentioned in the previous chapter: it was the individual's own life statement ('I'll go to the pub . . . and drink myself legless') that merits keen attention. This is a sad, life-denying attitude which required healing long before serious illness literally completed the job. As Shealy and Myss (1988: 23) insisted, leg problems do not always mean difficulty in standing on one's own. But in this man's case, it almost certainly did. A complementary practitioner, who happened to have known the patient as a friend since his early adult life, recalls the man using that chilling phrase throughout his thirties and forties, and his fearful reluctance to leave an unhappy marriage.

Many times we have no idea where the metaphor trail may be leading. It is the responsibility of the practitioner to enter into a form of explorative partnership with the patient, always one step ahead in being alert to unusual words or phrases used, and to the recurrent remarks or mannerisms which might be spelling out a form of code. When a patient presents with severe acne, for example, the practitioner could encourage them in counselling mode to talk about their emotional lives. The practitioner must note any 'victim mentality', hearing sentences such as 'I get picked on at work' or 'Dad always picks on me and not my sister'. Repeating the phrase to the patient can often yield a chance for further insight, when the patient might warm to her theme and elaborate with, 'Yes, it's not fair! I get so fed up, I go to my room and sulk . . .' And, no doubt, pick at her facial spots mindlessly as she broods over the unequal struggle for approval at home.

Consider the potent combination for this patient if the practitioner not only applies their primary skill to heal the skin eruptions but also provides a safe containment for the afflicted person to talk more about her victim role. The practitioner might offer an observation that they noticed a pattern repeating itself in her life – at work, at home, socially – and wondered if she saw any significance in that repetition? All this would gently unfold, in an unthreatening non-judgemental way, where active listening could facilitate key connections. In the best scenario, the patient would ultimately realize: 'I put myself up for being picked on', and decide to break the pattern, perhaps some months later reporting a less passive approach to her environment.

Early warning signs

Of course, key messages are not decipherable unless and until a skilled practitioner is open to reading them. Unfortunately, our society does not train us to listen for and interpret odd remarks dropped randomly into conversation. They remain just that – odd and random – and the speaker continues leading their life unaware of the destructive impact their belief system may be having upon their physical, or mental, well-being.

Luckily for one adolescent called John, his medical herbalist recognized danger signs when this young man casually remarked: 'I see life through a net curtain. Actually, I feel as if I am only half there most of the time.' The practitioner who, in her counter-transference, was experiencing feelings of being distanced by her patient, responded: 'Now you've explained how it is for you, John, I must tell you I have a similar sense. It's as if you don't want *me* to see *you* clearly. Perhaps you feel that to draw back the curtain would be much too risky?'

This proved a turning point in the therapeutic relationship. He showed relief that his 'secret' was out, that he could choose to take responsibility for the effect he had on other people, and that it was safe to explore now why he hid much of the time behind that curtain. He had cut off from living his emotional life to the full for fear of rejection and ridicule; in reality he was only half present. But that also ensured only half the pain when people he cared about showed him (what he perceived to be) negative feelings. As Clarkson (1989: 46) points out: 'Clients with schizoid personality traits usually show some significant disturbance of sensation by minimising or distorting the impact of internal sensations or external stimuli.'

This adolescent was reluctant to grow up, leave his mother and prove himself a man. Pirani (1988: 34) describes a similar Perseus figure 'who misses a father's cheerful encouragement and guidance to support him in his ventures into adult life'. He could well have stayed trapped behind his self-imposed isolating curtain for years, if not for ever. No one would ever guess how distant he really felt or understand why a relationship with him could never work. Serious illness, physical or mental, would probably lie ahead for this unhealthy, suffocated organic system. But the practitioner helped John find the confidence to experiment with expressing his true feelings. Central to their healing time together was her acceptance and sympathetic detachment, always without judgement.

The danger John faced was that he would almost certainly have exacerbated his isolation by continuing to take leisure drugs or ultimately in becoming an alcoholic; both forms of escapism serving the same, tempting solution as in hiding behind a 'net curtain'. This schizoid defence against the frightening realities of adult life is a well-worn route. In John's case, it was avoided (one hopes) through the skilful early intervention of his herbalist. It was she who noticed the warning signs and in due time outlined the alternative, 'fully living' choices open to him. This led to referring John to a counsellor to work on his reluctance to claim his manhood and risk being more present in the world.

The practitioner's timely insight, however, cannot be over-estimated. It is yet another illustration of the value of a combined approach to complementary practice, one in which it is essential to be skilled enough in counselling to know what might be going on, and what one's limitations are within that awareness. John's case is also a useful illustration of Mackintosh's (1981: 58) observation that:

> The nature of the interaction between the two parties [homeopath and patient] would seem to be of more importance than it might at first appear. One fundamental element is, I would suggest, a sense of a reality, for which the homeopathic focus provides the link that is shared by both patient and homeopath. In this atmosphere, where it is permitted to exist, the enhanced 'realness' can enable both parties to see and experience more clearly. Both parties can experience themselves as being part of a deeper reality.

The 'eyes of death' and depression

To see and be seen clearly has resonance across the spectrum of complementary practice, as it has in counselling and psychotherapy, indeed in all interactive relationships. To be aware of unconditional regard in the eyes of a practitioner has much the same significance (in its own context) as it has for a baby, safely wrapped in mother's arms and basking in the approval shining from her eyes. In a sense, the former is an adult extension of the latter, in that we are still, as it were, peering out from our safe place to check we are acceptable to the other.

When the messages are negative, the baby is not secure; and therein lie the seeds of future disturbance, the intensity of that depending upon many other internal and external factors. The exchange between practitioner and patient carries with it a similar, accepting 'holding' quality of unconditional regard (Carl Rogers describes this in his classic *On Becoming a Person*, first published in 1961), where the patient must feel safe and ready if they are to open up as never before. This could be their second chance, the missed opportunity come round again in which at last to see themselves mirrored, worthy and acceptable, in another's eyes.

In Sumerian poetry, the expression 'eyes of life' was used to suggest a seeing that is full of love and gives vitality. Jungian analyst Perera tells us also of 'eyes of death' in Sumerian mythology, eyes which are pitiless, not personally caring:

> To humans who are paralyzed with fear and lose sense of process and paradox, they can be the hateful glare that freezes life, like a mother's hate-envy that blights her child and makes an end of all beginnings – raw sadism and rage in its archetypal form. Or the eyes of depression, to which 'all looks dead'. They can be the eyes that transfix life, the projection of our human fear or rage, seizing a moment or an image and making it concrete and static. Such eyes bring psychosis; we see them in individuals suffering psychotic states, where the capacity to see through the tightly held fragment to the life process and spirit, in which the static frame inheres as a partial fact, is lost.
>
> (Perera 1981: 31)

Depression is almost inevitable for the child who experienced mother's eyes where 'all looks dead'. One psychotherapy client called Julia offers a particularly interesting illustration of how long-term, devastating damage was caused unwittingly by her mother, struggling with post-natal psychosis. Baby Julia must surely have experienced looking up at eyes where all looked dead, and as a result she learned in time to avoid looking at all.

So adept did Julia become at avoiding seeing into another's eyes that she appeared to be gazing intently at them whereas in reality focusing on the speaker's upper lip, the tip of their nose or chin. Her husband had never realized she did not know what colour his eyes were; and even her therapist was incredulous – on being told the truth – that for several years the two had conducted their professionally intimate relationship, chair opposite chair, without his appreciating that Julia's large, sympathetic eyes never actually looked into his own, as he believed.

The price Julia paid for this extraordinary avoidance mechanism was a constant feeling of being removed from the centre of life, a half-deadness that paralleled the deadness in her sick mother's eyes so long ago. Naturally, depression dogged her, suppressing her anger that she had not been welcomed lovingly as a baby, that her presence had been seemingly a source of irritation and grief. In therapy, Julia learned firstly to look at herself in a mirror; then into her therapist's eyes; then into her husband's and close friends' eyes. It was hard for her, and often she regressed to the habitual pattern. Eventually, she found the 'eyes of life' and of love, primarily for herself and finally simply for the joy of living. Her creativity flourished. Julia had found meaning in her mental illness and, as a result of that discovery, an end to the severity of the depressive episodes.

The complementary practitioner faces the task of trying – however limited the scope – to rectify this kind of terrible start in life. Of course, counselling their patients during treatment can hardly be expected to achieve a magical reversal, or anything resembling the successful outcome Julia's years in psychotherapy achieved. But, as we have already noticed, an adult patient can and will recognize genuine regard and grow on from there. The skill lies in identifying the trauma and that is why the practitioner's role as counsellor can be so important.

Body, mind and soul

Those who believe in holistic practice accept that there is more than the one-dimensional psychosomatic approach to health as embraced by science. The soul, too, they say, must take its place in a triad with mind and body. Drawing on Jungian analysis and Taoism, psychologists such as Mindell (1982) and Goodbread (1987) write of the body's role in revealing the true self. They describe techniques for amplifying body symptoms as signals from the higher self (our higher level of consciousness), and they suggest that a lifelong problem might be part of someone's individuation process: their search for psychological maturity.

Mindell (1982) stresses that a chronic symptom often serves

as a metaphor for a long-term emotional trauma. From what we have already seen, there is evidence to support this in clinics and consulting rooms universally. If, however, we allow chronic symptoms to express here-and-now information from the depths of the psyche, we need to realize it will not necessarily remove the pain; or, even if revelation does provide a healing catharsis, that pain may not necessarily go away. It might change in its intensity, or shift to another part of the body, or disappear for a while, only to reassert itself later. Mindell (1982: 69) puts it clearly:

> If you really get to the root of a process, then your projection can be integrated and the experience of your disease changes radically. If you are lucky, healing may occur. If you are even luckier, you will begin to grow. Even if your chronic symptoms do not disappear, they become friendly allies ushering you into a new phase of existence in which you behave as a whole and congruent person in the midst of a rich and meaningful life.

Meaning in illness nonetheless remains inconclusive, or elusive; significant for some, irrelevant for others. From the ancient religio-magical origins of our medicines to latter-day physicians and psychologists, meaning in illness is controversial and transcendental. Millenson (1995: 230) observes:

> As a complementary teleological perspective [a belief that events are pulled by a purpose towards a definite end] to our generally scientific practices, symbolism in disease expands our vistas beyond not just the frontiers, but also the accepted ground-rules of our science. Rejected as fantasy by some, condemned as a substitute for knowledge by others, and extolled as the ultimate ground of understanding by a few, meaning in illness is likely to remain an ever-fertile ground for both idle speculation and brilliant insight.

Summary

Illness might well be a path to self-knowledge and wholeness, but there is no definitive ruling on this and dangers abound in formulating simplistic ideas about why people get sick. Whereas some writers encourage us to believe every ailment is the result of our defective thought patterns and traumatized emotional states, others insist that this is a futile exercise. Both approaches may be true: we might usefully remember the value of paradox, if only to ensure a more balanced viewpoint. Some patients find comfort in being encouraged by their practitioner to find meaning in their illness; but practitioners should take their lead from the patient first, not initiate discussion which could prove counterproductive. A practitioner's timely intervention, on the other hand, could facilitate a major breakthrough in the healing process, even if their contribution is mainly to refer on their patient for deeper work. Counselling skills are essential in this respect, for it is in recognizing disturbance and in listening and observing sensitively in the first place that this sequence can be achieved by the practitioner.

The therapeutic alliance – one in which healing at all levels must be the first concern of those in the alternative *and* the allopathic world – is discussed in the next chapter. Although this book's primary focus is upon complementary practitioners adding counselling to their professional skills, it is inappropriate to ignore the GP's role in addressing the psychological aspects to healing. They experience similar difficulties, even tighter time constraints and the relationship challenges all healers face in meeting patients' needs as well as other difficulties of their own.

Chapter 6

The therapeutic relationship

Once in a while, something extraordinary happens in the consulting room. It has nothing to do with the quality of the hands-on healing, or any obvious aspect about an average, everyday kind of appointment. It is simply an in-rush of energy, a moment of connectedness which, in its hugeness, has a powerful effect upon both people in the room. Some practitioners speak in awe about this presence of energy; others, with a matter-of-factness that the phenomenon exists and regularly comes 'out of the blue'.

That it does manifest is unequivocal. One GP describes it this way: 'Every now and then, something gets touched on that is massively important to the patient. I get this instinctive feeling – I can't rationalise it – that something immense is in the room, an incredibly intense sense of something present, where everything else suddenly goes quiet' (Adrian Clarke, personal communication).

Perhaps this GP is speaking of a spiritual connection, a meeting of souls, the significance of which might be better understood by, say, the shamanic community. That it is metaphysical is beyond doubt to those who have felt the energy, since it is inexplicable in scientific terms; and that it has significance for a patient's own process is never in question. Put another way, we are discussing the relationship between healer and patient: the therapeutic alliance, a partnership recognized for millenia in some form or another and one which is just as important today.

There is no training for these encounters, nobody can be awarded a diploma in spiritual connection ability, and the occurrence is totally unpredictable. Yet when it happens, those affected feel buoyant, exhilarated, even humbled.

What on earth is it? Could it be some soul *reconnection*, an opportunity for reparation work at levels beyond our understanding? Millenson writes of the shaman's fourth causal realm, 'loss of soul'. Many indigenous people believe that illness is caused by loss of soul, and one of the shaman's main tasks is to undertake a journey to the 'other world' to search for the soul of the sick person.

> Loss of soul means to lose contact with the thread and purpose of our life, to stray from the path of inner harmony that is right and true for each one of us as individuals, to violate our own inherent nature. However complex, changeable and dimly illuminated that nature might be, ultimately its reality is sketched out by what proves harmonious or inharmonious to us in the day-to-day living of our lives. To delve into the meaning of illness is to step inevitably into the realm of life's purpose, to question the existence and nature of a higher Self that somehow is trying to manifest through us.
>
> (Millenson 1995: 210)

The Greeks have a word to describe this: *telos*, meaning aim, end or fulfilment. Teleology asserts that each one of us, like the cosmos, is moving towards a final goal. As Hillman (1996: 196) outlines: 'The goal may be defined in a variety of ways – reunion with God and redemption of all sins; slow entropy running down to stasis; ever-evolving consciousness and the dissolution of matter into spirit; a better life or worse; apocalyptic catastrophe or divine salvation.'

Hillman (1996: 8) reminds us of Plato's myth wherein the Greek philosopher suggests the incoming soul before birth elects the body, the parents, the place and the circumstances best suiting that soul's teleology:

> By preserving the myth we may better preserve ourselves and prosper. In other words, the myth has a redemptive

psychological function, and a psychology derived from it can inspire a life founded on it. The myth leads also to practical moves. The most practical is to entertain the ideas implied by the myth in viewing your biography – ideas of calling, of soul, of daemon, of fate, of necessity . . . The rest of the practical implications swiftly unfold: (a) recognise the call as a prime fact of human existence; (b) align life with it; (c) find a common sense to realize that accidents, including the heartache and the natural shocks the flesh is heir to, belong to the pattern of the image, are necessary to it, and help fulfil it.

The healing moment

Is it possible, therefore, when practitioners suddenly experience an intense, unexpected surge of energy in the consulting room as they counsel a patient, that they and the patient are somehow experiencing a tuning into some teleological design? Could they be 'switched on' to an unpremeditated meeting of souls whereby the healer says the right thing at the right second, when the patient is ready to hear it, and a moment of truth, congruent with *telos* (and Jung's concept of synchronicity), is somehow being enacted? Of course, no one can answer this definitively, and Hillman's view is as good – or as bad – as we choose to perceive it. He is not alone in his convictions. Ram Dass and Gorman (1985) and Myss (2001), among others, have written extensively on the soul's 'contract' and theirs is not too bizarre a concept, if we take the wider view and allow for other dimensions, or levels, in our lives.

In acknowledging the mysterious powers of the placebo effect, for example, where real pain can be relieved by a sugar pill because the recipient believes it will, we are already halfway down a path leading to the mystical, or the alchemical. Acupuncturist Richard Bertschinger comments: 'It's always *more* than we can conceive. You can put things into place, as it were, create the stage and arrange the props there, but then the drama has to unfold on its own, without ego being present.' He goes on:

> I work for the NHS some of the week and I watch patients with a serious disease stop treatment, yet they get better;

while others stay on treatment and they get worse. It is a complex issue and it is not just what happens in the room. Our job is in waking up that self-healing within the individual. People do miracles all the time – their brain is capable of switching off pain, for instance, when their toothache goes away because they are absorbed watching television. But then it comes back! Why? We still don't know what the mechanism is that throws the switch. But we do know that a soldier's phantom leg, blown off at the knee in battle, can still hurt – impossibly – years later.

An old lady came to me in distress some 30 years after she had undergone surgery and no one could accept that she was still in pain. In talking with her I learned that she considered she hadn't needed the operation and was angry that she had been treated badly. Of course, I used needles in my own treatment but I believe it was more through listening to her and believing she was experiencing pain as she described that the real healing came about. As in Gestalt therapy, she had at last found closure in her life, when a practitioner finally acknowledged her emotional trauma. The old lady had reconnected with her life script and as a result she told me she felt transformed. She now uses far fewer drugs and is much more physically active.

(personal communication)

The placebo can work negatively too: this is evidenced by the anecdotes we hear of voodoo deaths where healthy people die because they believe the power of the witch doctor's spell. This reverse of placebo, called nocebo (meaning noxious rather than pleasing) is present when a physician offers a patient a poor prognosis in a pessimistic way, failing to balance the diagnosis with a positive reminder of the patient's unique inner strengths and resources. Suedfeld (1984: 159–64) noticed that the nocebo can be seen clearly in experimental studies where the normal effects of potent drugs are sharply diminished when patients are misled into believing they are receiving placebos. Skevington (1995: 261) sums up the debate on the whole fascinating subject, concluding:

Quintessentially, [the placebo effect] is a socio-psychological phenomenon, because it integrates the patient's beliefs and expectations about the treatment received with those of the person who administered the treatment and the situation or context in which this exchange took place.

Recovery and the life force

The life force is often referred to when sick people get well. We say, 'They have such a strong vital force, no wonder they've made a good recovery', and few would query the essential meaning. Yet most are at a loss to explain precisely what that force might be, other perhaps than a manifestation of their genetic inheritance. If the teleological factor cannot be accepted, another way to understand the consulting room phenomenon described earlier might be to regard the upsurge of energy as electrical. Chiropractor Katharine Jenking points out:

> We are electromagnetic, sensitive beings as well as beings made of flesh and blood. What happens with that extraordinary 'meeting' is perhaps an example of synergy – that is, the sum of the whole being greater than the parts – and one which, of course, occurs spontaneously. When I work with patients I try always to keep a positive outlook, push difficult thoughts out of mind (such as if the person on the bench smells, or if I've had a bad day) and I believe that approach helps. Whether it works in conjunction with the electromagnetic force I cannot be sure. When I touch someone's body I need to remember and respect they are human beings. If positive thoughts help the healing process, then so be it. I don't impose my beliefs on my patients. It's true that sometimes I find myself saying the right thing at the right moment and healing seems to be the end result. Occasionally, it's almost hilarious how everything just 'fits together', where we both know there is *more* going on in the room. I certainly don't pooh-pooh anything that has not been proven – nor do I want to push my luck in imagining there is something special going on.
>
> (personal communication)

For every complementary practitioner who accepts the

mysterious or inexplicable aspect to their work, there are others who conduct their practice with little or no acceptance of such phenomena. Their patients seem satisfied, they run a thriving, professional business and perhaps they do not wish to consider the possibility of the existence of other dimensions, such as Hill-man has suggested (1996: 8). However, the quality of the thera-peutic alliance *and* that rare, energetically charged 'meeting' between practitioner and patient, seem to be linked.

A good alliance cannot depend upon such phenomena, but it seems to enhance the relationship; a sign, perhaps, of con-nectedness at a spiritual or universal level that we cannot under-stand. Being open to what comes certainly appears to be the better way forward for practitioners, even if parts of the route are incomprehensible. Concentrating, where appropriate, on one obvious means to connectedness – as counselling offers – unquestionably helps the therapeutic relationship flourish. Knowing the skills to access a patient's inner world, via the methods we have already examined, is clearly a major element towards this end. Unfortunately, counselling and psycho-social methodologies in the twentieth century were not part of most practitioners' training programmes, particularly those in the allo-pathic field.

Sympathy is not enough

In mainstream medicine the GP often feels limited in the kind of psychological medicine they are willing or sufficiently know-ledgeable of – to offer. This was the story leading up to the new century, when most allopathic practitioners could offer sympathy and reassurance only, along with the diagnosis, prescriptions or referral to a specialist. The paucity of the typical GP's psycho-logical tool kit can be explained in part his or her professional emphasis on finding a physical pathology for every illness. If nothing emerged to diagnose and treat, there was little else to be offered.

This was where the alternative, or complementary, world of healing began to claim a significant proportion of the patient population. Alternative practitioners, primary disciplines apart, not only had the time to devote to their patients but brought to the consulting room a concentrated presence and attention that patients had obviously felt lacking in the NHS. This became the basis for a strong latter-day patient–practitioner relationship, out of which the *vis medicatrix naturae* (as Hippocrates called the healing power of nature) could manifest, in tandem with the alternative practitioner's own treatment. It is undoubedly that to which Richard Bertschinger refers in his anecdote of the old lady (see page 60 above), where the key to her return to some semblance of health lay in being 'heard' at a holistic level, rather than being prescribed more pain killers by her doctor.

It is the quality of the practitioner, their 'being', integrity and openness which all appear to be central to the success of the therapeutic relationship. If medical students in the previous century were educated largely as scientists, then the new century appears to call for a melding of scientific and holistic approaches. The latter stresses growth and acceptance of the self in ways the allopathic model largely does not. As Mitchell and Cormack (1998: 113) comment:

> The revival of interest in complementary medicine, insofar as it relies relatively less on technology and more on personal meaning, can be seen as part of a shift away from the emphasis on rationality, science and technology ... Life energy should be used with a good background knowledge, otherwise it may produce haphazard results or cause more harm than good. Intellect without life energy cannot directly affect the patient's self-healing forces and may therefore only lead to temporary and perhaps superficial results in treatment and then only for those patients with acute rather than chronic illness.

West Country GP Roy Welford, like Adrian Clarke, is involved in primary care work where their health centres offer complementary services to patients. He sees major change ahead:

> Allopathy *has* to meld with alternative. It would be unrealistic to think they cannot and we would be doing a disservice to the patients if they did not. Complementary therapies work and they are cost effective. Case studies have proved, for example, that counselling is often better than

anti-depressants and counsellors are now available through almost every practice in the country. But there is still a lot more talking to do before NHS managers are prepared to commit funding towards other fields in complementary practice.

Of course it is preferable if we can enable and empower the being of the person to heal themselves, and generally people do seem to prefer to use modalities that address inner healing levels too. To engage with patients at soul level is very satisfying. You can see it happening and that can be quite fulfilling, for they often do come with a need for spiritual help. It's important we are open to support patients – we can't just patch them up with medication when they are trying to deal with big issues in their lives. And that is where the quality of the practitioner (no matter which discipline) and the work they have done on themselves in terms of personal development, is so crucial. I have had no formal training in counselling – I learned 'on the job', both as a doctor and a homeopath, using empathy and a non-judgemental modality of assessing what's going on. One of the privileges of general practice is that we get to know more about our patients from other sources – family, partners – without asking questions, of course. When we are told things it is helpful for us in building up a bigger picture. With the third party's consent, we can use the wider view sometimes in the therapeutic encounter – and this approach is not normally open to a counsellor.

(personal communication)

Balint, a psychoanalyst writing in the 1960s, addresses another useful concept for doctors (which he calls 'the cumulative consultation'), in which the bigger picture can develop within just a few minutes after meetings spread over years on a one-to-one basis, similar in quality (though not in time frame) to the counselling experience. Balint has firm views on the need for a restructured medical training programme. He states:

It is generally agreed that at least one-quarter to one-third of the work of the general practitioner consists of psychotherapy, pure and simple. Some investigators put the figure at one-half, or even more, but, whatever the figure may be, the fact remains that present medical training does not properly equip the practitioner for at least a quarter of the work he has to do. Although the need for a better understanding of psychological problems and for more therapeutic skill is keenly felt by many practitioners, they are reluctant to accept professional responsibility in this respect.

(Balint 1964: 107–17)

The 'white coat' effect

Mention 'white coats' and the association is manifold: usually, the listener will conjure up images of authority figures, pursuing their important business in hospital, laboratory or surgery contexts, though this image is perhaps more a throwback to the last century. Certainly, there is a widely held belief among the medical staff in doctors' surgeries that patients' blood pressure levels tend to rise if they know they are going to be tested; the 'white coat' effect operating here is an anxiety-based reaction. It is not without significance that some doctors refer to the test results with the caveat 'white coat reading' unofficially attached to them, acknowledging how much fear can affect tension.

Richard Bertschinger, an acupuncturist, wears a white coat for reasons far removed from the need to assert his authority. Pointing out that butchers wear white coats, too, and that science does not have the monopoly on them, he stresses that in donning his own he feels he is doing his job. He adds:

> I'd really like to be working in the wilds, making fires, letting people drop in for free healing . . . but if I go into town, expecting patients to pay, it makes sense to wear a coat. It is also clean (covering everyday clothes) and we must not forget that in acupuncture we are piercing the skin, a medical procedure.
>
> (personal communication)

A white coat can be a metaphor for power. As GP Adrian Clarke points out:

We doctors do have immense power – it's inherent in every consultation and sometimes that's the way our patients allow or like it. The paternalistic 'white coat' is alive and well, although in a more subtle role and it will never be dislodged: the 'good Daddy' (or 'Mummy') transference is still needed by vulnerable patients who must feel they can trust us. It is almost inevitable that the parent/child relationship informs the doctor/patient transaction. This has its therapeutic advantage and its disadvantage. Where someone needs to 'grow up' – become psychologically mature – then my status can prevent them doing so. At times, I've felt it would have been more therapeutic for certain patients to lose their temper with me! However, in the medical consultation I bring my view of illness, my role and expectations of my role. Patients in turn will have their expectations of me: this is the background against which I perform the counselling content of my work, despite the obvious time constraints. It's clear to me it's impossible for GPs to counsel as other professionals can but it is also obvious we are obliged to do it all the time.

I am married to a counsellor, and therefore my understanding is that the core of counselling lies in the relationship between counsellor and client. If positive, it provides an environment in which the client can be examined, change, grow, whatever. Some GPs share this view with counsellors and complementary practitioners. But doctors have a body of knowledge those others may not have: we are experts, giving us extraordinary power over our patients. It is frightening the extent to which I am trusted and it is a sobering thought. If I make mistakes, people can die. We offer an upbeat, pragmatic image yet there is very much a shadow side to being a GP. There is this socially high status, along with the fear of falling from that pedestal – and this is a doubleedged sword. We have a lot to lose if we make a dreadful mistake . . .

(personal communication)

An empowering relationship

Empathy can be experienced at its most profound level when the doctor or complementary practitioner is able to disclose parts of themself, both in sharing their own feelings arising in discussion and also in offering interpretations and even striving to help the patient find ways to solve the problems emerging. The practitioner's ability to reveal themself as a person can touch the patient and deepen the therapeutic relationship. GP Adrian Clarke says: 'I find sharing uncertainty – if that is what I am feeling about the diagnosis – is nowadays allowed by patients, because they want to be involved, part of the process. It's important that I stay self-questioning enough and not lose a sense of balance. For example, a woman patient once complained that I was being too "psychological" about her anxiety over an issue. We came to a shared understanding and we parted on good terms – and I acknowledged to her that I get it wrong sometimes' (personal communication).

Such an open attitude towards the work, where a practitioner learns from his mistakes as well as successes, is a prerequisite for today's healers. The scarred and wounded are among the best placed to attend another on their journey. Millenson (1995: 258) posits:

> Illness is the vehicle, and the practitioner's caring attention and presence are the catalysts for healing, the power of which ultimately lies within each individual . . . Somehow the therapeutic alliance established between patient and practitioner provides impelling towards wholeness. Yet it is not the practitioner who heals, it is the relationship.

Thus we see that practitioners need to clarify their own views on life and living before they can be of real help in any deep, or transformational work. In their 'being' holistic healers – be they medical or complementary – must be aware that it is primarily their job to find and address the causes of imbalance, or the reasons the patient is suffering from what shamans call loss of soul. The placebo effect, witch doctors' snake oil, even the (literally) swallowed prescription, carefully torn in uniform pieces and taken four times a day by a misapprehending foreigner delighted with the remedy, demonstrably can speed the healing process. The practitioner's job is in part to clear away the obstacles to its efficient operation, and in part to be there for, and to attend to, the patient during the time that the restorative force operates.

Summary

The therapeutic alliance is a partnership between healer and patient which has existed for millennia. The quality of that relationship appears to be affected and enhanced by the quality of the healer's own inner world, their openness to what comes, their 'being', empathy and authenticity. It seems important for them to be clear about their views on life and living, and to have some understanding of their own psychological wounds before they can expect to work at deeper levels of healing. The power of the mind, linked with the extraordinary fact of the placebo (and nocebo) effects, and the patient's innate ability to access the healing power of nature, are astounding phenomena still not fully explored, although they are acknowledged by scientists and mystics alike.

Given that the quality of the therapeutic relationship is enhanced by the well-being of the practitioner, the next chapter explores problems around safeguarding and maintaining that well-being. This will apply not only to the context of ensuring emotional and spiritual nourishment but also to matters of protection, both professional and psychic.

Chapter 7

Perils and psychic protection

We were holidaying in the Tuscan hills. A small group of us basked in the idyllic grounds of a beautiful old farmhouse hotel run by an English couple. The mood was relaxed and carefree until, one day, a newcomer arrived. Also English, she was a woman on her own and yet she made her powerful presence felt immediately. Then, as if systematically, she began to destroy the gentle atmosphere in various subtle ways. No one could quite put their finger on how she was doing it. Yet within a day, everyone felt ill, drained or angry and longed for her departure. What was really happening? The answer almost certainly lies with psychic contamination: an unseen, destructive energy which can create havoc.

This can happen in the workplace, the community, even the therapy room. It is an energy often linked with buried rage or fear, an unacknowledged shadowy darkness of soul which all too easily finds discharge and relief by unconsciously downloading on to others. But we should note how Myss (2001: 158) explains this energy: 'The word *shadow* itself suggests a dark, secretive, possibly malevolent countenance that looms in the background of our nature, ready to do harm to others as well as to ourselves. A much more appropriate understanding . . . is that [the shadow aspects] represent the part of our being that is least familiar to our conscious mind.'

Thus, if anyone had challenged this woman, pointing out their resentment that she had invaded their space with intrusive conversation, it is more than likely her response would have run along the lines: 'But I was only trying to be kind/friendly/helpful . . .', such protestations being accompanied by a look of baffled concern. Yet her behaviour was directly responsible for quarrels breaking out between couples (including the proprietors) as a result of her divisiveness. Some guests cancelled dining in, for fear she might be sitting near their table on the terrace; another woman was reduced to tears because she had been 'caught' for an hour in the newcomer's psychological web – an advice-laden monologue – and felt trapped beyond her control. The proprietors later declared privately they would never accept a booking from this disruptive visitor again.

Such a scenario is not unfamiliar, although perhaps an extreme example of how one person can negatively affect others. Psychic contamination can be pervasive, covert and sometimes even toxic, often leaving its distressing impact long after we realize what is going on when we can do little to avoid it. Many experienced practitioners learn how to safeguard themselves before, during and after encounters with those patients who contaminate their room. This is achieved in various different ways, which are discussed in Chapter 8. It should be understood, however, that practitioners are most at risk when they do not appreciate that harm might be being done to them, albeit unintentionally. They may feel drained, depressed, or 'out of sorts' with themselves but they fail to realize that at some level they have been emotionally 'vampired'.

Ignorance and arrogance

There is always the danger that unaware therapists or practitioners will believe they have the strength and intelligence necessary to ward off psychic bombardment. But, as Rioch *et al.* (1976: 3) noted: 'If students do not know that they are potentially murderers, crooks and cowards, they cannot deal therapeutically with these potentialities in their clients.' In other words, this disowned shadow realm in our unconscious minds requires conscious acknowledgement, for without it we cannot recognize the destructive energy in others.

Psychological distress, as the woman in Tuscany exemplified

in her frantic need for attention, is as infectious as a viral illness. As Pietroni (1986) points out, doctors and nurses dealing with patients who have a physical infection have learned the importance of protecting themselves from catching their patient's infections and they take precautionary measures, such as protective clothing, or barrier nursing.

> It is equally necessary for workers involved in dealing with 'psychological distress' to be aware of how infectious that can be. How much 'protection' is it possible to develop without losing sensitivity, openness and empathy that are necessary tools to continue to work with people? For many workers in the caring professions this is a constant battle, and an increasing number find themselves requiring counselling, psychotherapy and relaxation to enable them to continue working.
> ... There is often an unhealthy collusion between workers and clients and an even more unhealthy need on the part of the worker. He (*sic*) may consider that he has been drawn to this profession through a noble and altruistic wish to help the needy. However, on closer examination he may find that he needs the helpless more than the helpless need him. He is then locked into a vicious chain of events that will eventually cause him to face his own need and helplessness.
>
> (Pietroni 1986: 164)

Facing our own needs and helplessness can be a painful experience, although it is a necessary one. It is only when this recognition has taken place that a practitioner can be regarded as 'clean' and therefore safe, not only, of course, for themselves but also for the welfare of their patients. Hawkins and Shohet (2000: 5) explain it well:

> [Self-supervision] begins with appraising one's motives and facing parts of ourselves we would normally keep hidden (even from our own awareness) as honestly as possible. By doing this we can lessen the split that sometimes occurs in the helpers, whereby they believe they are problem free and have no needs, and see their clients as only sick and needy.

If the destructive holidaymaker had been a client in psycho-therapy (instead of, incidentally, a self-taught counsellor, as she alarmingly claimed), her rage would have been better processed, and not left to simmer unchecked. Guests might have picked up *some* of her mess, but not at the daunting level we and others experienced and suffered in various ways.

Attacks can be harmful

Psychic attacks are driven mostly by an unconscious grabbing at another's resources, as in the need for warmth and comfort; or to share a load or devour voraciously in order to fill a vacuum; or as a means of killing time, giving the perpetrator a buzz of some sort. Though unwelcome and unpleasant, these 'thefts' of energy, replacing the positive with the negative, are probably scientific-ally unprovable, but that does not make the perceived results of them any less injurious. Who, after all, can afford to give away their precious life energy? Healers such as Maureen Leigh who channel it for their patients act as go-betweens. Leigh told me: 'I work as a conduit. I would never claim healing occurs through my own life force' (personal communication). Healers learn to guard this life force, or chi energy, very carefully at all times (witness the Bible account of Jesus of Nazareth sensing that someone in the crowd had touched his robe and drawn energy). Leigh herself experienced a dark attack of horrifying strength, yet she survived it by understanding that she needed to offer light energy to help disperse it.

Psychic vampiring is not limited to the consulting room. According to the psychoanalyst Dion Fortune, it can happen at work, within a family, between a couple, even between mother and child. She writes:

> I am of the opinion that what Freud calls an Oedipus com-plex is not altogether a one-sided affair, and that the 'soul' of the parent is drawing upon the psychic vitality of the child. It is curious how aged Oedipus cases always look, and what little old men and women they are as children. They never have a normal childhood, but always are mentally mature for their years. I persuaded various patients to show

me photographs of themselves as children, and was much struck by the elderly, worried expression of the childish faces, as if they had known all of life's problems and burdens.

Knowing what we do of telepathy and the magnetic aura [energy field], it appears to me not unreasonable to suppose that in some way which we do not as yet fully understand, the negative partner of such a rapport is 'shorting' on to the positive partner. There is a leakage of vitality going on, and the dominant partner is more or less consciously lapping it up, if not actually sucking it out.

(Fortune 1981: 57)

Fortune uses the term 'parasitism' to describe rather than 'vampirism' which I have used, and she insists that psychic parasitism is 'exceedingly common' (1981: 58). Perhaps it lies behind what sometimes happens in a consulting room, when a practitioner starts to feel drained and miserable.

Contagious contacts

One-time City high-flyer Susanne Preiss notices similar symptoms among the world's top management figures who come to her workshops on de-stressing techniques.

They find themselves in career situations that feel stagnant and dead end. They feel hopeless and that means they cannot fully develop their potential. This *is* contagious. It spreads like a virus and manifests in non-clarity, sleeplessness, psychosomatic symptoms, irritability. I recall a woman lawyer struggling with all of this and in trying to protect herself from her colleagues' own distress she created an imaginary psychic 'balloon' into which she thought she could hide in the workplace. The balloon didn't work – she still felt daily contaminated by her peers' depression and fears. Her own low energy level had made her overreact, get her life out of proportion and all too easily she fell victim to their psychic contamination.

(personal communication)

Psychotherapist Dina Glouberman, co-founder of the Skyros holistic holiday centre in Greece, feels concern about the term 'contamination', although it is used so frequently. She suggests a better word might be 'transmission', where the negative connotation is replaced by a more positive one. 'If I offered to a client in therapy, for example, that in the counter-transference I was feeling contaminated, then there is the danger my client might feel judged. The reality is that we are all connected to each other at some level. On any one day, we might feel better in the presence of another human being; on the other hand, if they are in an empty hole, we might feel sucked into it.' She goes on:

> My experience tells me I usually pick up on people's unconscious material more than on their conscious self, however cheerfully they may present themselves. So I might say to my client: 'I notice I'm feeling depressed, which I was not feeling when I first came into the room. Are you perhaps feeling depressed today?', and that can prove quite creative within a session and is an example of what I call transmission. The positive side of this interconnection is that we practitioners are often able to 'tune in' and pick up certain things as a medium does, or even clairvoyantly. The secret is to learn to tune into our clients in a conscious, positive way. This is a natural talent we all have and can learn to access.
>
> (personal communication)

Roger Woolger, a Jungian analyst who lectures internationally in regression therapy and shamanic healing, has another slant to offer when he suggests that many of our energy problems, obsessive issues and persistent complexes often turn out to be old or ancestral spirit energies trying in vain to speak or act through us to resolve unfinished issues not of our, but their, making.

> I frequently encounter and remove unwanted and unhappy spirits. Some spirits originally attach to us in childhood, others after a family member's death. We live in a heavy, dense psychic world and parts of Europe, America and the United Kingdom carry an accumulation of grief from wars, slavery and persecution. Spirits that hang around usually died as a result of sudden death, bomb blasts, hospital

deaths, traffic accidents, that kind of thing. Millions of souls do not have an opportunity to let go (unlike those who die peacefully) and they stay around the earth's psychic field, attracted by some kind of resonance. We don't use words like 'possession', we say 'attached'. Usually a sensitive, psychic member of a live family – or, indeed, the ambulance driver, the nurse, anyone who unwittingly offers light and warmth – can attract that attachment. Our unconscious has an energy field, a band around us, and it is to this energy field the spirits are attracted.

(personal communication)

Woolger points out that the word 'protection' implies a need to fight off. Admitting he has worked on rare occasions with demonic possession ('demonic means, in my view, a psychic oil slick, full of concentrated nastiness'), there is, nonetheless, no such thing as good or evil spirits: 'It is instead a question of light and heavy energy. When heavy or dense energies accumulate in the human aura, or energy field, the Peruvian shamans' practice is to concentrate on collecting them in their psychic belly, or stomach (they call it the *poqpo*), digesting them and deliberately sending them down and back to the Earth Mother, Pacho Mama who, it is said, loves to eat them' (personal communication).

McNeely (1987), also a Jungian analyst, envisages future therapeutic practice evolving into new dimensions of thought. He suggests:

> Just as we now see psychosomatic processes in physical and mental-emotional images, so will we be able to visualize and sense kinaesthetically [an ability to notice body sensations] what is occurring in the body of the analysand, and this will be our automatic and natural response. We will see consciousness fill out spatially within and beyond the physical body as individuation [psychological maturity] takes place and is expressed in the subtle body or dreambody.
>
> (McNeely 1987: 107)

One cranialsacral therapist who already embraces this approach in her body work, and also as a psychotherapist, is Brigitte Scott. Scott trained with Roger Woolger in shamanic healing and believes that sometimes dead people fail to recognize what has happened to them and that they may need help to move on to their ancestral home in the spirit world. She describes a patient called William who complained he had felt under psychic attack for the past several weeks. Scott decided to make an intervention that is currently unorthodox in most clinical settings.

> William spoke of his dead grandfather, an alchoholic who had died of terminal liver failure: he knew his Grandad had been terrified of dying and suspected that he had subsequently attached himself to William's own energy field. I suggested we dialogue while William lay on the bench and closed his eyes. Through an intuitive sense of his grandfather's responses, using this role-playing technique, we discovered another reason for his fear of dying and why he might have attached himself to his grandson. The reason was that his late wife would be waiting to punish him.
>
> I asked William: 'But what would Grandma really say to him when they were reunited?' And his response immediately came, 'Oh, she'd forgive him – I can see her wanting to show him some evidence of that forgiveness . . . She is going up and kissing him on the cheek . . . They're walking away together, happy and reconciled. Grandad is telling me it's okay for him to leave now. This may sound corny, but it is what I am somehow aware of watching. In my mind's eye, like a dream world, I have witnessed this take place and really feel something has happened to release Grandad'. After this, we still had to attend to William's body in order to integrate the experience, both at physical and energetic level.
>
> Thereafter, my client never again complained of the stomach cramps and deep sadness which had triggered the dramatic session. It's my belief that trapped discarnate entities want our warmth and energy and they *will* zap it. Healers who are able to see people's auras can detect scarring on our energy field, a manifestation – for those who are clairvoyant – of the actual damage being done when entities attach and draw from us.
>
> (personal communication)

Watch for the danger signs

These are some accounts of psychic bombardment from the living, with the possibility of contamination from the dead, if we are to acknowledge with Roger Woolger and others the unrecognized needs of earth-bound spirits. There is another professional peril that nobody would dispute, a phenomenon occurring in pandemic proportion throughout the helping professions. This epidemic concerns physical and emotional exhaustion, or, to give it its twenty-first century name: burnout.

Complementary practitioners are among those particularly at risk, precisely because they take a caring approach to all aspects of their lives. At some point their spirit of generosity dries up; there is nothing left to spare. Giving out that extra effort in counselling their patients while at the same time attending to their healing techniques can tip the balance: resentment sets in, or perhaps anger, disgust, despair. Again, it is a matter of energy: whether leaking out, transmitted or, indeed, vampired. However we describe it, the crux of the disturbance is an energy imbalance. Homeopath Cassandra Lorius (2001: 85) writes:

> I could not face the thought of hearing one more problem, which is not how I usually feel about the privilege of sharing people's life stories and discovering the surprising and creative ways they deal with their challenges. Energy might be dissipated because of the ways our own emotional problems can get stirred up during our attempts to care for others. Sometimes it is due to an overload of negativity and problems which erodes our optimism; at other times it is due to a crisis of conscience, when we are no longer sure we are doing the right thing. Whatever the reason, problems suddenly become burdens and we feel the strength of our own needs. Our burnout is telling us that we can no longer leave those needs on the back burner. They must be attended to.

Susanne Preiss suffered burnout so badly she had terrifying panic attacks at night, exacerbated by a constant sense of being in a state of red alert against some life-threatening disaster. A successful advertising executive at the time, she worked sixteen hours a day, driving herself to earn the love and admiration she learned to recognize she was then craving from her parents. From her home in Germany, Susanne told me: 'I left my job and travelled with my husband to China, wanting to be with him but also because I was still in a very bad state. It was there, in a park, I saw a group of people doing some sort of exercises which were led by a master. I had a restless feeling inside, looking for something to help and not yet knowing what could help me. But these Chinese clearly had something they valued and practised. I remember I almost felt angry because I lacked what they had got.'

What she was witnessing was an ancient form of healing exercises called Qi Gong (pronounced 'Chee Goong') used in China for over three thousand years and today an increasingly important part of traditional Chinese medicine as it is practised in the West. Susanne sought out her own master and learned how to direct the flow of chi (Qi) along the meridian system to various positions, organs or acupuncture points. Her mental and physical health began to improve and the panic attacks lessened. She also found a German-speaking counsellor in the Philippines ('I'm a big fan of counselling') and eventually she felt well enough to decide to join the healing professions. She started her own company, designed to help business executives cope with stress, using the meditative breathing and muscle toning exercises she had discovered in China.

Paradoxically, Susanne suffered her burnout before she switched from industry to healing: today, she keeps her health and inner balance in better fettle. 'I do still get occasional panic attacks, but they are far less frightening now that I know just what they are: a symptom of my having failed to listen to my body's needs. If I ignore the little signs, the body finds a way of saying "I'm not working for you any more . . .". I have finally realized that I must use personal discipline to practise the Qi Gong exercises every day' (personal communication).

Listening to the message

When Dina Glouberman burnt out, she did so after achieving a lifetime's credit list of successes. She had just celebrated the publication of her first book, resigned from her university lecturing post in psychology, was running Skyros holidays, seeing private clients at home, and embarking upon a formidable project in launching a new magazine.

> One day I walked out of the house and couldn't go home. I stood in central London's Picadilly not knowing what to do. The noise was too loud to bear and my head hurt badly. The next day, I had absolutely no energy. My brain ground to a halt. This was the start of a long-term health breakdown. For years after I burnt out, my exhausted body went on strike . . . I'd cry if I had to write a letter. In my groups, when we took turns at finding images of our lives, a typical one for me was: 'I am a ghost in the attic'.
>
> (Glouberman 2003: 19–20)

It took seven years for Dina to recover her full energy and, just as Susanne Preiss experienced, that did not mean an end to the panic attacks and other symptoms which marked their respective crises. Roger Baker noticed a similar pattern in his own encounter with panic attacks. In his book on coping with panic he describes how, after retiring to bed one night, his heartbeat, sweating, tension, breathing all seemed to be speeding up. As a psychologist he could readily identify his distressing symptoms as anxiety and not some physical disorder. But that did not stop them happening.

> Somewhere around this stage, after all my efforts to calm down had failed, fear seemed to step in. Looking back now, the event is organized in my mind, and I am presenting a much clearer picture of what happened. At the time it was unclear, chaotic and very, very unpleasant. Many of the fears related to the future.
>
> They were all of a type we could call 'supposing' fears: 'supposing' my body carried on at this rate, I could never get to sleep. I couldn't do my job properly. I would lose my job, be made redundant, not able to support my family. 'Supposing' my body carried on at this rate, I would be continuously aware of my heartbeat and breathing and not be able to concentrate on the more detailed things one needs to do as a clinical psychologist – such as listening carefully to patients, picking up clues from what they said, working out what to focus on next in the session, giving a lecture or writing an

article. 'Supposing' I was continuously aware of my
heartbeat and breathing I would have no peace, and be in
constant misery.

(Baker 1995: 134)

Interestingly, in keeping with these different examples, Baker's
own account of his panic attacks offers more than symptoms, in
common with Glouberman and Preiss. He told me: 'Professionally
I had been feeling stale. I was doing an awful lot at work, one
factor being a new area which was at times difficult and distressing. I had been in the same job, in the same city for fifteen years. I
couldn't see anything bright or new in the future and thought
"things will go on much the same", without expecting any psychological problems. In retrospect, I realize I was in a trap but
did not properly realize the situation at the time' (personal
communication).

Sick and tired

We hear the phrase 'I'm sick and tired . . .' in many contexts, but if
we apply it to aspects of our life, our work, our relationships, we
might reach a better understanding of what it is that these high-
profile people are trying to communicate in sharing their personal
experiences. Basically, when we enjoy whatever it is we are
engaged in, we revitalize ourselves. And, if the occasional trauma
emotionally knocks us, we deal with those disturbances success-
fully enough to be able to continue on our way. Rachman (1980:
51) defines this as 'a process whereby emotional disturbances are
absorbed, and decline to the extent that other experiences and
behaviour can proceed without disruption'.

It is when we fail in that emotional processing, or, to put it
another way, when our heart goes out of the situation, when we
are bored or overstretched for too long but soldier on nonetheless,
it is then that we become candidates for burnout. There is, however, a positive aspect to this current epidemic. As Glouberman
(2003: 57) suggests: 'Burning out may literally save our lives by
stopping us before we suffer a more serious or fatal illness. On
another level, burning out saves our life by showing us how
and when our life lost its old meaning and by forcing us to do

something about it. We may not save our old life, but we can free ourselves to be more fully alive.' There is a strong message here for complementary practitioners about the significance of burnout precisely because the holistic approach to health embraces the key issues of body, mind and soul working in harmony.

In my own case, I was driven to work long hours not only as a psychotherapist but also as an administrator and lecturer when my partner and I moved to a large house in the country in order to run residential courses there. For several years, the plan worked smoothly, just as we had hoped. But a large, old house needs expensive maintenance and we were both getting tired. My practice fulfilled me in every way – but the additional stress of many weekend retreats and workshops throughout the year was more than I had originally bargained for. Headaches, pelvic inflammation, then panic attacks about the cause of (and no relief from) that mysterious pain began their warning signs; but still I persisted. After all, there were obligations to meet, bills to be paid and I had always been able to count on my stamina and ability to cope. Then, one dark winter's morning, I realized I was walking down the corridor almost literally out of my mind (it is variously called disassociation, splitting or depersonalizing).

I had no sure sense of my identity and in a disembodied way fell to wondering who lived here, what they would think if they should find me wandering uninvited about their home. It was a frightening time, replicated in different ways over months, yet these episodes happened only when there was no structure to the day. I worked well with my clients, was fully present and 'in my right mind'. Then came another shock: I noticed a remarkable synchronicity with two of my clients who were enduring comparable personal ordeals. Neither knew of my own, of course, for the professional reason of boundary-keeping. But here the possibility of psychic contamination might usefully be reintroduced: for this was more than coincidence. It has never happened before, nor since, in nearly twenty years' practice. The question is, however, who infected whom? Was this somehow *folie à deux* (madness for two), or was it another illustration, as Glouberman has suggested, that we were, at some level, connecting with each other's distress? Certainly, we were all emotionally and physically exhausted and therefore wide open to another's unbalanced energies; but the reality of our different illnesses was unequivocal. Which came first? Who did the transmitting or receiving?

As a postscript, it must be added that all of us fully recovered. Both clients as well as I came to recognize in time the richness and intrinsic value of our difficult experience. The two clients saw it in some way as necessary to their process, and that their burnout (or breakdown) did indeed slowly turn them round to face and accept what needed to be changed in their lives. They are not alone in their assessment: my life also has altered course, and as a direct result of those anxious months.

Summary

Psychic contamination appears to be a reality. It affects us in many contexts, unexpected and unpredictable; probably because its energy emanates from the unconscious mind where suppressed, unacceptable elements lurk in the shadows. Because they are unacknowleged and usually subtle in impact, they can cause havoc and it is important to understand that contamination can be injurious, as infectious as any virus. There is also the possibility that we can be affected by other, less down-to-earth energies which sap our well-being and influence mood. This may require professional help to release any unseen 'attachments'.

Burnout and psychic contamination could be linked, so that they are sometimes indistinguishable from each other. Because we are connected energetically, one person's exhaustion might be reflecting another's, or even causing it through exacerbating an existing condition. Burnout is a state of emotional overload, yet it can also herald massive and necessary personal change. It is reaching epidemic proportions throughout the world, occurring mostly in the workplace as stress and demand levels rise.

What is clear is that there is great need for self-care, which is discussed in the next chapter. There, I examine various methods and practices recommended by practitioners in diverse areas of complementary healing.

Chapter 8

Dealing with difficulties: finding support

Imagine a patient walking into the consulting room who reminds us of the overbearing woman in Tuscany, described at the start of Chapter 7. She might be one of those 'heart sink' patients who interfere, demand, bully and wheedle their way into ruining an otherwise good day's practice, just as the Tuscan holidaymaker ruined the group's well-being while she stayed at the hotel. We might guess that bad vibrations are about to invade the consulting room, and her shadow is likely to cast a blight on the therapeutic relationship and the immediate environment.

But there is neither time nor inclination for a practitioner to embark on any deep work. The patient is here for the treatment she or he expects to receive. Any attempt at psychological healing would probably prove counterproductive; and besides, this is no case for counselling skills. As we have already seen, those skills teach us when *not* to move in, and intervention of any sort would be inappropriate for an angry, frightened client, unconsciously bent upon pulling others down to join them in a disturbing inner world.

The best plan in this kind of situation is to suggest a competent therapist to whom the patient could turn ('if ever you felt the need to talk with a professional') and thankfully bid goodbye until the next appointment. But how does that leave the practitioner feeling? The chances are that they might want to thump the wall, fumigate the room, throw open the windows, or do all three. Probably the latter only would be possible within the time (and practical) constraints of a busy practice. A more workable solution might lie in taking daily preventative measures, first thing in the morning, leaving what brief opportunity is available to attend to emergency cleansing of the room after a difficult session has ended.

Salt, for example, can absorb depressed or 'heavy' vibrations in a room, just as its crystals absorb moisture out of the atmosphere. Some practitioners claim that a bowl of fresh water left near their patient can do much the same job, but they insist we remember to tip it down the sink each evening. Smudging dried sage in the consulting room (by blowing out the lighted leaf and waving it about to encourage the embers to smoke) has cleansing properties and creates a bracing, pungent scent. Lemon grass essential oil has similar properties.

Therapists find their own favourite methods over the years, using various aromas which best suit them, or they simply remember to wear pure silk against their solar plexus as a less obvious safeguard. William Bloom, who runs workshops on psychic protection, suggests stabilizing or rebalancing the energies in a room with the use of objects representing the classical four elements – earth, water, air and fire – each in a corner of the space. A cup of salt would represent earth; a glass of water, itself; burning incense (or a fan) represents air; and a lighted candle, fire. Bloom (1996: 69) comments:

> Within minutes of placing the objects you will find the atmosphere beginning to settle . . . Many sceptics could not believe that something like this would work, but I encourage them to try it and they are always surprised at how obvious the change in atmosphere is.

Shake about a bit

Giving yourself a good shake can release energy that is blocked, or glued into you. Bloom points out that some people could suspect they are being energetically attacked or vampired when, in fact, they are merely experiencing energy which is stuck and failing to move.

Moving and shaking your body will free up your own frozen
energy, as well as moving any that belongs to someone or
something else . . . I have worked with hundreds of medical
people, therapists and counsellors, and I think they are crazy
not to take at least a minute's break between clients. In this
minute they can practise some small ritual for their own
personal psychic health and hygiene, even if it is just opening the windows and stretching. Ideally, they ought to take
several minutes, open the window, stretch, shake, walk and
wash their hands and sit quietly for some seconds to centre
and integrate their energies. This kind of practice is relevant
to anyone working intensely with people in any business,
service or profession.

(Bloom 1996: 72)

Running water can be helpful in cleansing psychic mess. Of
course, medical students and nurses are taught that washing is an
integral part of hygiene; but what they may not have been told is
that, according to Bloom and others, flowing water helps wash
away the energy of the previous patient. Medical herbalist Ned
Reiter has this to offer: 'Make a ring with your hands after turning
on a cold water tap. Imagine all negativity, pessimistic energy
flowing down the arms and hands and through the ring into the
sink, flowing down into the earth. It's a ceremony, or ritual, I
perform daily and it works for me' (personal communication).

Many colleagues use a 'zip up' personal protection plan, in
the form of an imagined armour, whether it be a wet suit, yogic
egg shell, balloon or heavy medieval battle shield. We must not
forget the power of mind magic here: if we believe and focus
strongly enough, our thoughts should do the work necessary to
safeguard against unwanted energies. Conversely, Reiter's own
philosophy echoes that of Roger Woolger, in that he *opens to*,
rather than *wards off*, any perceived invasion. Reiter says:

I try to be non-judgemental and the opposite of tightening
up against an attack on me. Like aikido or judo, we neutralise
attack without harming the attacker. Then again, do keep
control of the situation – don't let the patient take control.
Don't be afraid of saying 'I have to make my own professional decisions' to the patient who is determined to tell you

> what you should do, or use on them. And yes, sometimes it
> is not possible to face treating someone: hairs stand up on
> the back of my neck and I will sit through the whole initial
> session and then respond with something like, 'I don't think
> herbalism is for you', or 'I don't think I'm the right prac-
> titioner for you'. I charge them no fee, of course. It is import-
> ant to be honest with ourselves in realising what we can and
> cannot handle.
>
> (personal communication)

Reiter, who is president of the National Institute of Medical
Herbalists, meditates daily, cycles miles in the summer months
and watches carefully over his health at all times. If he experiences
what he calls vampiring patients, he will fall back on his Zen
training to cope with them.

> I do a quick scan, asking 'what's happening to me here?' If
> there's a tightening up and a sense of wanting to tell the
> patient to shut up and get out of my life, I let my chi energy
> sink down into my centre and just observe what this person
> is doing. I make sure I am breathing properly, then I do not
> engage: I don't try to send bad energy back and I refuse
> inwardly to be a target. The only way it is possible for others
> to take your energy is if you are colluding with it happening.
> (Reiter, personal communication)

Patients can be troublesome in many different ways. They
can smell unpleasant: for example, with body odour, cigarette
smoke or foul breath. Practitioners naturally struggle with trying
to ignore it but many acknowledge dreading the reappearance of
certain patients. Chiropractor Katharine Jenking however, deals
with it in a positive way. She told me that when she touches her
patient's body, she always tries to think good thoughts, 'whether
[the patients] are lovely, or if they do stink dreadfully. If I have
had a bad day, I try to remember they are human beings, asking
for my help and paying for it. It must make the world a better
place to hold positive thoughts like this.'

On the matter of personal protection, Jenking realises that as
an occasional home visitor she could be at risk. She dons her white
coat for two reasons: firstly, it provides a small physical barrier

from the hygenic point of view, and secondly because wearing a working coat gives her a sense of a psychic barrier. 'It all helps to create the atmosphere of remaining professional. The more "props" I have the better. After qualifying, I bought the best equipment available to show the patient unconsciously that I am doing *my* best and therefore expect them to do *their* best, both in responsibility and in looking after their health' (personal communication).

Violence and abuse

Violent situations, sexual provocation and professional litigation are serious potentially damaging areas for any complementary practitioner, whether they work from home, in patients' own homes or as a member of a clinic. At all times, it must be remembered that the practitioner should act with decorum, respecting the rules of boundaries (discussed in Chapter 2) and taking every possible care to ensure their own personal safety as well as that of their patients. Panic buttons are increasingly being installed in home settings, and their use for therapists working alone, particularly in an empty house, is advisable.

Respecting the boundary-keeping ethic is always important but never more so (in terms of personal safety) than when therapists work from home. Avoid any hint of inappropiate intimacy. Photographs, family snapshots, framed personal messages on show in the workroom can give out another message entirely: namely, the practitioner is *not* professional. These accessories are (or could be interpreted as) seductive clues to private identity, virtually inviting further intimacy. 'That's a nice looking man – is he your husband? ... Oh, so you haven't got a partner, then?') is an obvious example of a first step into difficult territory, should the practitioner find herself facing a would-be Casanova or someone on the lookout for a friendly liaison of any kind.

Harmless enough in themselves, private details should be avoided wherever possible. A wiser alternative is to use plants and neutral pictures instead. Moreover, it is in the interests of the 'blank screen' backdrop necessary for the therapeutic relationship and that rule should apply to the choice of ornaments in any consulting room; with the exception, however, of a GP's surgery, where homely touches can reassure patients of all ages, and a 'blank screen' impression is not an integral part of the work.

Sexual assault upon practitioners by patients fortunately is rare: we could look for the presenting reason as one explanation for this. Men and women who are depressed, needy, frightened or in physical pain come for relief from their distress, and are not likely to represent a threat. Psychotic, or borderline psychotic patients, on the other hand, can prove unnerving and this is where a handy panic button, ringing outside to alert neighbours and passers-by, can bring peace of mind for the practitioner. It might be sensible to make other arrangements for treatment sessions with unpredictable patients, or at least to arrange for someone else to be in the house during their visits.

Violence already done to a patient before they present for treatment is on the increase. Those practitioners whose speciality lies with body work are more likely to notice the tell-tale signs of bruising. In the complementary field, osteopaths, chiropractors, masseuses and aromatherapists are among those professionals who must be aware that suspicious marks on an undressed body might be evidence of home abuse. Patients try to hide bruising and usually deny they have a domestic problem. But it can be a professional requirement to know about body scars and whether, for example, rebalancing would cause more, rather than less, trauma in any treatment. Questions may need to be asked before any work can start. One chiropractor told me:

> I will probably open with some kind of casual question like 'Do you play a contact sport?' Then, if there's no reasonable cause for the bruising offered, I might pursue the questioning further, but gently. A patient of mine once responded 'I do have a rocky relationship with my partner . . .' and then I was able to ask if she had anyone she could talk to about her difficulties.
>
> I make sure I have a list, or directory, nearby to offer the patient names and telephone numbers of, say, local refuges, counsellors, even the police. Once I told a woman that I was worried about the amount of physical trauma she often presented. She burst into tears when I went on to say it looked to me that someone was heavy-handed with her and

that she should contact an agency for help. She rang me later and thanked me for putting her on the right path.

Regarding the sensitive issue of possible child abuse, it should be remembered that a practitioner is culpable if they do not take action when they suspect their young patient is being physically abused. (Sexual abuse is harder to detect and cannot come into the remit of this chapter. However, all practitioners are obliged by law to inform the relevant authorities if they have any doubts or fears.) Reporting concern to the social services is vital, and it is also crucial to keep ongoing notes, facts and records in case of any future litigation and the need for evidence.

Bruising on children need not necessarily mean abuse, of course: but if there are deep markings round the wrists or on cheeks, for example, these could have sinister significance. What then can be said to the parent, or guardian? Practitioners need to tread carefully here: there is always the danger that any adverse comment could make the abuser angry and defensive, and that they will take it out on the child later.

Suicidal patients

Adults for whom life has lost all meaning can be a risk to themselves. The key factor in indentifying a suicidal patient lies in the degree of hopelessness they demonstrate. This can be learned through observing their body language – their expressions, gestures and posture – and whether the various signs indicate true emotional collapse. Slumped shoulders, failure to make eye contact, wringing hands, tears and sighing can all be vivid clues about the patient's state of mind. But many mental health workers have been fooled by taking these symptoms at face value: they *could* instead paint a picture of today's misery only. On the next visit, the patient may present buoyantly, their crisis apparently an ordeal of the past; but it could be a clue, perhaps, that they were unconsciously bringing from childhood an ability to flick the melodrama switch whenever it suited them. That in turn might provide an opportunity for counselling.

But how do complementary practitioners recognize the difference? True depression does not come and go within brief intervals: deep melancholia is experienced by the observer as a heavy, dark blanket ceaselessly enshrouding the sufferer; it is a dungeon of despair from which there seems to be no escape, no end in sight. If a practitioner should happen to see the same patient a fortnight later and the symptoms are unchanged, then there is cause for alarm. Some of the symptoms exhibited by a clinically depressed person are:

• daily mood of sadness and despair
• self-reproach, low self-esteem
• sleeping too long, or too little
• low energy, slow speech and thinking
• inability to concentrate
• weight gain, or loss
• lack of interest or pleasure in life
• tendency to dwell on bad news
• suicidal or thoughts around death.

When a combination of these symptoms persists over several weeks, then there may be reason to suggest a patient sees their doctor. Many complementary practitioners make it an integral part of their practice to ask new patients for the name and address of their GP. Psychotherapists and counsellors also need to know to whom to refer if they are unsure of what medication a client has been prescribed and if, or how, it might affect their overall mood. Doctors are usually happy to respond to professional written queries of this kind. They would obviously wish to be informed if their patient seems currently at risk, in case the problem has slipped through the net at the surgery and its severity is not yet recognized.

How do we know when to act on behalf of a seriously depressed person? One sure sign of impending disaster is if a patient talks of ways and means of committing suicide, and how they actually plan their own death. Others are if they admit to trying suicide before, and if suicide runs in their family. These are generally regarded as the determining factors in deciding suicide risk. No one can be dissuaded from taking their own life if they are resolved to do so, but the area which must concern the practitioner lies in encouraging their patient at least first to seek professional help, perhaps calmly pointing out how their death will affect relatives and friends, that their dreadful despair may prove only a temporary crisis and that life may one day offer more meaning for them.

This is hard and difficult work. It can bring down a practitioner in much the same way as psychic contamination can: we are, after all, in the presence of dark energy. Sitting with a suicidal patient, for whom life is hopeless, is a profoundly painful experience for the witness too. Seeking help for that witness (the practitioner) is of paramount importance in order that the load becomes shared behind the scenes. Yet whereas most would agree on the priority in this situation, too few practitioners realize that peer support and supervision are fundamental needs at all times throughout their working life. The concept of supervision for therapists who are long past their professional requirement for a mentor (as in the early stages of practice) is comparatively new.

The value of support

Like the medical profession, complementary practitioners, once qualified, have tended to consider formal oversight of their work as superfluous and, indeed, unwarranted. It smacks of inefficiency; of being monitored; even of weakness of character if they are known to be unsure about coping with practice problems.

Roy Welford, a GP, observes: 'Primary care doctors have informal ways of working off stress, such as playing sports, and I rather think most do not take advantage of formal, peer supervision. Instead, they take unscheduled time off, retire early, or they burn out. There is, too, of course, a high rate of alcoholism and drug abuse in our profession, which would point to the high levels of stress they are suffering.' Welford discovered long ago as a homeopath the value of peer support and regularly uses it in his primary care work. He adds:

> One of the benefits in working in a busy GP surgery is in being able to offload our troubles and grumbles on to the partner in the room next door. It's good to feel it's acceptable to a colleague to discuss an annoyance, provided there is agreement and the opportunity to do so. Doctors are viewed by the general public these days as too easily accessible: they

barge in and insist on seeing me, and that can be really disruptive and annoying. Some patients do not act responsibly or considerately enough. It can be very frustrating having to juggle priorities.

(personal communication)

Another problem doctors face is one of isolation, if they do not themselves recognize the value of peer support. Reflective practice, as GP Adrian Clarke describes it, is essential if 'shutting down' is to be avoided.

My wife is a counsellor and she is the main influence on me in encouraging me to stay with this self-reflective thinking. Through reflective practice, we learn integrity, openness and humility. When I started, I was a single-handed GP and got very sucked into it, obsessed and focussed on doing an enormous amount of work with little self-awareness. That came to a head when my mother died – I was getting more and more stressed (I didn't *do* vulnerability very well!), and eventually I began seeing a clinical psychologist, a lovely chap, and that proved extremely helpful.

(personal communication)

Treating patients year after year can mean a backlog of unmet needs of the practitioner's own, regardless of the particular discipline in which the practitioner has qualified. If those needs remain unsatisfied they can undermine a sense of competent professionalism, and this inevitably has a negative knock-on effect upon their patients. As acupuncturist Isobel Cosgrove points out in the British Acupuncture Council newsletter:

Supervision refreshes, inspires and gives us a chance to satisfy our professional needs. It relieves the tension of working on a one-to-one basis; it asks me to be accountable for what I say and how I behave with patients. Families, partners, friends and colleagues can all provide at least some support in the form of listening time at the end of a long day with patients. But a supervisor is also a practitioner, with years of experience in dealing with situations like our own, who knows how to recognise early signs of burn out and take appropriate action, how to be less self-critical, how to reinforce feelings of self-confidence, enhance self-esteem and to clear the psychological and emotional debris which collects during a working day.

(Cosgrove, 1997)

Maintaining high standards for patients and for the practitioner has become an integral part of increased maturity in the acupuncture profession in the western world; but, as Cosgrove insists, with increasing maturity comes increasing responsibility. 'We have enjoyed our freedom, independence and individuality of approach to work and professional life in general for the past 30 years. When I began offering supervision training courses, some people thought at first it meant policing their work. Feedback was seen as threatening. It is taking a long time to pursuade the profession that feedback is actually helpful, and positively contributes to one's life as an acupuncturist' (personal communication).

A new feeling

When acupuncturist Jane Robinson joined Cosgrove's training group, she embarked on the initial weekend session feeling it was something she ought to do, even if she failed to like it ('a bit like taking medicine'). But by the end of the weekend, she knew she had made a good decision and looked forward to the next with quiet relief, tinged with excitement. She told me:

After 25 years in practice I thought I had learned how not to be stressed by the job. Indeed, in many ways I had, but being in practice can be a lonely existence, and I have come to discover how useful and supportive it can be to work in a group of practitioners with whom I am not also in business. I have been able to examine issues within my practice, many of them small but significant, and gain help from the rest of the group for ways to resolve them. Even better, it is being part of that support for others and discovering that many of their issues are ones I also share and maybe have not articulated before.

(personal communication)

A significant insight emerged for Robinson as the course developed. Where once she would have found herself, among her own acupuncture peer group, presenting as exhausted and on the verge of burnout to sympathetic colleagues who understood what she was talking about, now, as a member of a national supervision course which seeks to teach as well as to support, she experienced a new feeling of lightness and freshness. She reports her present viewpoint like this:

> I have a means of controlling that near burnout state, and it is a great relief. I feel I am in the driving seat at last, the practice isn't bigger than me. I am no longer trying to 'rescue' my patients from their various tragedies and pains; I am willing to look at the bigger issues going on within the practitioner–patient relationship; I don't constantly judge myself as not being good enough; I am more aware of boundary issues and the patient–practitioner contract; I am attending to my own needs and feel much stronger within myself. I know I need to stay engaged with this process.
>
> (personal communication)

What emerges from these accounts is that there is a real need for professionally run supervision training in all disciplines throughout the complementary healing world – and in the allopathic community – which should principally address care of the self. Such structures do appear to have the edge on peer group work, though they should certainly not supersede it. Ideally, of course, there is a place for both systems of support.

Another term for supervision is 'mentoring'. Mentoring training, such as that offered by Cosgrove and others, covers issues of confidentiality, boundaries, projection and transference, building support networks, contracts, time and money management, and how to prevent burnout. Fortunately for would-be student therapists, some universities and colleges are increasingly offering supervision, or mentoring, training on their complementary therapy course curricula; but there is still a long way to go.

Not all alternative therapy students have such learning opportunity, and in some areas of healing a possible danger could lurk in poor quality primary training, later being reinforced in peer groups by graduates' own uninformed input, however sincerely or kindly meant: a case of the blind leading the blind, serving no one. Those originally 'trained' at occasional workshops spring to mind here, where depth and rigour cannot have had the chance to unfold, given the shortness of time allotted and the lack of continuity of practice overview.

But there *are* avenues open meanwhile to practitioners who may not yet have found a rigorous training course, supervision group or supervisor who has been trained rigorously. It is possible, for example, to find a qualified group leader from the national professional directories, listing psychotherapists and counsellors, practitioners who have been permitted by their own accrediting body to teach or supervise (see the appendix to this book). Contact someone listed locally, discuss the possibilities of their leading a group of complementary therapists, irrelevant of the discipline (the dynamics will be familiar, even if the speciality is not) and consider next setting up a small group of fellow workers. Find out if they, too, are interested in the nurturing, support and psychologically educational content that such a regular gathering could offer.

Why supervision is necessary

Let us acknowledge that supervision has little to do with teaching the actual skills that pertain to any particular discipline: those should have been fully covered in the training years. Naturally, the ideal arrangement would be in introducing a knowledgable and experienced practitioner in the same field of work to the newly formed group, someone who has additonally secured supervisory, or mentoring, skills. But the healing community overall is still too low on such resources. Even in the psychotherapy and counselling world, trained supervisors are quite rare: we 'old timers' have been forced in the past to seek out more experienced colleagues to supervise our work. But fortunately for us the story has slowly begun to change over recent years.

Moira Walker and Michael Jacobs began running two-part five-day residential courses for counsellors and psychotherapists in 1990 at Leicester University and then later in the West Country. Neither had received any specific training in supervision, as none was available, but, like Cosgrove, they developed a model and a structure of training which hit upon the right formula from the start and inspired colleagues to graduate and take their experience and new insights out into the workplace throughout the British Isles. In their training structure, they realized the intrinsic value of many issues:

> Creating a supportive environment is vital to our own model, but this does not preclude being challenging, although without being threatening or persecutory . . . However, if the supervisee perceives challenge as punitive, this must be explored, as must any other difficulties that arise. This means acknowledging the real relationship that exists in the supervisory dyad . . .
>
> (Walker and Jacobs 2004: 10)

Walker and Jacobs stress the value of acknowledging and working with the supervisee's own difficulties. Although the role of supervisor is different from that of a therapist, supervision can be therapeutic without becoming therapy.

> It can be caring and offer valuable support. However, we also believe in providing a firm and reliable container to the supervisory process, particularly where there are boundary issues in the therapeutic work being presented. It is neither contradictory nor necessarily problematic to create clear and appropriate boundaries and offer support to and recognise the whole person; on the contrary, these are complementary and essential elements of the process.
>
> (Walker and Jacobs 2004: 11)

As we have already seen, finding supervision in one's own locality or speciality may not prove a simple task, nor may it be possible to trace a competent leader who, though untrained in a particular healing discipline, has the necessary qualification to facilitate a group. It could all seem just a bit too daunting. There is, too, a recognized resistance to searching anyway: 'Why should I spend more money and energy on something that may not really be much use?', is the kind of response often heard.

Mitchell and Cormack (1998: 141) cite time lost from

clinical contact as one reason for complementary practitioners failing to secure personal (paid) support for themselves. Other reasons included negative effects upon family life, in terms of expenditure and time away from home. These authors confirm that some practitioners were inhibited from admitting failure (in any form of supervision work) 'through low self-esteem and loss of pride' and voiced a suspicion that support systems would prove emotionally costly as well.

This is a sad reflection on the quality of the training bodies who graduated such practitioners, presumably failing to instil in their students enough sense of personal worth and identity to feel empowered to seek contact with others as an ongoing form of support and help.

Setting up peer group supervision

If neither proficient supervision nor professionally facilitated group work is accessible, then setting up a peer group is certainly the next best move. There are, of course, caveats to bear in mind. It is all too easy, for example, for peers to use the time available to chat rather than discuss in a consensually agreed, contained way; to be lax about arrival and departure; to give too much space to the most talkative, when others need their turn; to 'therapize' inappropriately; or indeed, to *avoid* intervention for fear of causing offence. As Walker and Jacobs (2004: 50) stress:

> In order for peer supervision to work, it is crucial to have certain basics in place. Establishing the time and timing is essential: how long the group will meet at each session, how often will it meet, as well as agreement on starting and ending promptly. Having an appropriate room that is always available, confidential and of sufficient size is important. If the room is in an agency and has to be booked and paid for, there needs to be clarity regarding who is responsible for making the arrangements and how the room is to be funded.

Clarity of purpose and commonality of needs and aims give a good chance of success. How large should the group be, and how regularly should it meet? Complementary therapists, largely unbound as they are by their accrediting bodies' failure to require post-graduate supervision, are in a different position from that of counsellors or psychotherapists. Most, but not all, sections of members registered with the United Kingdom Council for Psychotherapists are required to present evidence of supervision while in practice and to seek reaccreditation after a few years; and the British Association for Counselling and Psychotherapy guidelines stress the need for ongoing supervision in order for their members to be reaccredited annually. So the format can be fairly random for alternative therapists.

Until professional supervision is mandatory, a moral need exists, however, for practitioners to develop their own ideas for useful peer supervision. Apart from using group time for discussion, they might consider devising experiential exercises or introducing role-playing techniques. The whole point is that they should find colleagues to share new learning opportunities, address difficulties or other problems together, and pay heed to warning when burnout is spotted by fellow carers, and – most importantly – to take heart from encouragement.

Summary

Patients can be difficult in all sorts of ways and practitioners need help to face those difficulties. Three ways in which a practitioner might find such help are: (1) by finding a trained supervisor, (2) by becoming a member of a training course in supervision or mentoring, or (3) by running a peer group, ideally seeking out a qualified supervisor from the ranks of psychotherapists or counsellors to facilitate that group, used as they are to the dynamics involved. Meetings are valuable, even if they can be arranged only occasionally: thorny issues arise in any community and we all need to be confronted at certain times in our lives. In addition, group members can make those meetings a part of their ongoing personal development. However resistant some practitioners might be to giving up time and finance for this (as yet) non-mandatory branch of good practice, they are likely to find the meetings valuable for their professional well-being. It is a matter of personal integrity and self-responsibility, both for themselves and for their patients.

In the final chapter, we look – not surprisingly – at endings in therapy, including the problem some practitioners have discovered in never *quite* concluding their working relationship with patients, and what the implications are for such unresolved closures.

Chapter 9

Endings and never-endings

The classical symbol of the snake swallowing its own tail (the *uroborus*), suggests, among other interpretations, the creation of a perpetual circle, but it has significance for us as we contemplate endings in therapy. Is an ending always a desirable objective? Does failure to end imply weakness, or does it instead point to deeper levels of commitment to the life process and all that this involves? Should the cessation of physical pain, a satisfying disappearance of specific presenting problems, necessarily mean an ending to the overall healing relationship?

One patient's answer will be different from another's. The reason for this depends quite properly upon where, along a long list of priorities, they see their own position. The patient's level of self-awareness, their bank account, and other commitments will all stack up to influence their response to the above questions; furthermore, what they say one day could change to a new viewpoint at some other time. We are left without any clear answers. So perhaps we should look instead at the wider picture of endings and never-endings.

In order better to understand the issues involved, we might need to agree that the word 'therapy' must be seen in its generic meaning, covering the spectrum of holistic healing, physical or mental (although they are of course intertwined). A patient may conclude a series of sessions with her acupuncturist after several weeks' successful treatment and never seek out alternative help again; someone else might wish to remain a patient for the rest of their life, either in preventative, or maintenance, treatment or because it simply feels right for them. In counselling or psychotherapy, elegant but brief work can be achieved in a relatively short time; or clients might stay in therapy for many years and still not feel ready to stop exploring their inner world. As Ernst and Goodison (1981: 293) observe:

> We see therapy as a continuing process. You may want to work on yourself in different ways throughout your life. This is likely to mean that at different times you may want to work on pressing conflicts or distress, or explore a new aspect of yourself . . . People were often surprised to find that after five years we were still active members of a self-help therapy group. This is probably because they see therapy on a medical model where a sick person enters treatment and leaves when she is 'cured'. In our group we all felt that we had more control over our lives and more satisfying experiences than five years previously, but we still found that we could use our group for discussion, support and for doing therapy together when we needed to.

These authors make it clear that therapy in all its forms does not seek simply to 'fix it' for clients and patients: the holistic way is infinitely more complex than the medical model, and herein lies the confusion about an appropriate conclusion. Sometimes, a wish to leave hides a fear of going deeper, of avoiding challenge and upsetting the status quo; it can reflect a pattern set up in earlier life of dreading a sense of entrapment (indicating, paradoxically, the need to remain in therapy until that unconscious material has surfaced and been cleared). Alternatively, if the reverse seems true, and the client clings to the safety of therapy and abhors the idea of ending, then working through dependence issues can be crucial to the therapy's final stages.

Maximizing our physical health, attending to our emotional well-being and respecting the spiritual content of our journey all sound ideal for the patient; choice, after all, remains largely in their hands. But where does this leave the carer, seemingly tied to the treadmill for the rest of their working life because so many of their caseload choose to stay indefinitely, or to return from time to time for further long spells? The prospect can be daunting for the complementary practitioner who, unlike their mental health colleague who may envisage an ending to their patients' quest for psychological maturity, might expect to greet familiar patients for decades.

It can be daunting, too, for the family doctor, for whom some patients form a needy, lifelong attachment. As GP Adrian Clarke explains: 'Neat endings are unusual – I'm holding everyone's psyches for years. Many patients have been with me for over eighteen years and I have some ambivalence about that because for a proportion of the time I am knackered. In the complementary context, with shorter episodes, practitioners are nonetheless in a similar position to GPs with their ongoing workload: there is never a psychic completion, and that is artificial' (personal communication).

Developing a tolerance

It may be necessary for practitioners to develop a tolerance to the never-ending quality of their relationship with some of their patients. This assumes that they do feel reluctant to keep treating them and secretly want to free up appointment time in order to meet newcomers and refresh their professional life. Most therapists enjoy working long term and are content with the knowledge that their practice is valued; but it is not always the case, particularly if they feel concern about 'overuse'. Is their patient proving a bit too clinging, for example? When a neurotic dependence is obvious, then weaning a patient off treatment might be indicated.

This may, however, prove more difficult than it sounds, as GPs in particular are aware. Some patients have a genuine hunger to turn to a parent figure in their loneliness. Complementary practitioners, too, know – and undoubtedly also wish to respect – this form of their patients' needs. But distinguishing one from the other – the neurosis from the real – is quite difficult for the therapist and they should check what the counter-transference (see Chapter 1) is saying as a guide. Is a sense of being greedily devoured at each meeting, instead of feeling genuinely sought after, showing it is time to remove those neurotic hooks and say goodbye?

It is quite proper to do this, even when dependence is not actually the issue. Sometimes a practitioner can work for a long time to try to remove some blockage without success, and a farewell in this case is implicit even though no one is to blame for the stagnancy. It is right (and ethically required) to admit the treatment is not working and to suggest other practitioners who might more effectively reach and heal the problem. Not only is this form of professionalism good practice but it also serves to improve a reputation for integrity among alternative therapists who have in general suffered adverse publicity in the past. This has often been as a result of the actions of irresponsible mavericks in the complementary community, themselves justifying bad feedback and public disgrace.

One example of this was reported to me, where a radionics healer, using a 'black box' diagnostic machine (placing either a blood spot or hair strand on a slide and tuning into the patient's frequencies) tried to convince a newcomer she was seriously ill with cancer. The therapist nearly persuaded her to sign up for countless treatment sessions, charging high fees. Devastated with the 'diagnosis', the patient in shock decided next to seek private medical advice, with all the attendant tests, and was subequently told there was no sign of any cancer, or pre-cancerous tissue. This happened many years ago: she is still in good health. Her story may not have reached the national press, but it alarmed a wide circle of her friends and did little to impress them to trust complementary practice.

This episode also emphasizes the urgent need for more regulation throughout the alternative healing world.

Dealing with endings

Somewhere in the middle ground between the never-ending patient and the patient who terminates their treatment prematurely, without warning or explanation, we find the bulk of patients. These are the people who have reached a natural break in their healing, are ready to go it alone or, indeed, may be forced to move on for other reasons, such as relocation. Gratefully, they show their appreciation, take their leave as expected and the ending culminates with good feelings on both sides.

Every day, practitioners face the possibility, or actuality, of different quality endings, and good feelings on both sides are not guaranteed. Practitioners can never be sure whether a patient in mid-treatment will return, however apparently content at the point of leaving. In the interests of professional rigour and deliberately safeguarding against this uncertainty, many psychotherapists make it a rule to contract initially that, no matter what happens (with the obvious exceptions of serious illness or death), an unsure client who wants to leave agrees to carry on for a few more sessions. This is in order to work through the issues arising and to leave both therapist and client with some sense of completion, however minimal.

The rule has much to commend it. The problem for complementary practitioners, who largely do not operate with this caveat, lies in the parallel to be drawn between the medical model and their own form of healing discipline, namely that when a patient does not feel encouraged by physical improvement (their only evidence, after all, that the healing method is working), they may withdraw without discussion and look for help elsewhere. In mental health work, a different criterion applies. We sometimes measure success only when presenting symptoms get *worse*; we wait, sitting it out while the client suffers the pain of regression, even blaming us for failing them. Perera (1981: 70) describes this waiting time as a valuable affirmation of their suffering, a necessary period of endurance:

> Complaining . . . does not, first and foremost, seek alleviation, but simply states the existence of things as they are felt to be to a sensitive and vulnerable being. It is one of the bases of the feeling function, not to be seen and judged from the stoic–heroic superego perspective as foolish *qvetching* and passive whining, but just as autonomous fact – 'that's the way it is'.

Then (and often only then) can the client start to get better. All this is an integral part of the process towards emotional healing. It is the main reason psychotherapists and counsellors seek the security of the agreed 'contract' against abrupt termination; in time, the client pulls through their difficult passage and moves onward, ideally now trusting whatever might happen. The complementary healer, on the other hand, is neither qualified for, nor usually expected to cope with, such dark episodes. If regression has occurred spontaneously, for example, when the transference (see Chapter 1) has convinced a patient that Bad Mother, or Father, has failed them yet again, this can be hard to take.

There may have been some physical improvement, but the patient will be loath to admit it, leaving the practitioner feeling bewildered and hurt. (Remember the counter-transference!) Hurt, impotent feelings can easily indicate the patient's original carer experienced a similar relationship with this angry 'child', still unconsciously furious that no one could get it right and make her feel better. The best way forward here might be gently to suggest: 'You seem rather upset that we don't appear to be making good enough progress – but I'd like to encourage you to hang in there a little longer: we *are* working through a lot of layers, and it is early days yet to consider giving up on the treatment.' This, at least, shows a degree of awareness, of containing the predicament calmly and offering the patient a way forward acceptable to them. Incidentally, this can also prove to be the first time that Bad Mother/Father has had the opportunity to transform into Good Mother/Father. Perhaps the patient's history included being rejected as uncooperative, being difficult, or obstinate. The only means at her disposal now lies in doing the rejecting herself, making the carer feel useless, punishing them as perhaps the patient once felt punished. It is important to understand this dynamic: it can take a measure of the sting away when we are on the receiving end of another's scorn.

So, in offering an open, honest assessment to encourage the patient onwards, the practitioner might simultaneously be repairing some of the damage laid down in that person's childhood, as it resurfaces in this comparable setting where primal distress is central and perceived failure to alleviate that distress instantly (as a child demands) affects the new 'parent' role negatively. For the adult within that person to discover kindness, consideration and humility in their practitioner may prove a hugely significant turning point in their lives.

It can also forge a deep sense of connection to the healer, and make the true ending phase all the more meaningful as the patient prepares to move out into the world again, less distrustful and less wary of betrayal. It is a deeply satisfying moment for any practitioner to know that change has occurred and that healing at many levels has touched their patient. It is, however, a time of mixed feelings, by no means clear cut despite any rejoicing and satisfaction. Completion can presage a period of mourning, another loss in a string of losses, for such is the natural cycle of life and death, even when we view this symbolically, as we see in the *uroborus*. That image tells us of slaying the self yet paradoxically bringing life to that self; in fertilizing and giving psychological birth. In Jungian terms, this describes accepting and assimilating the opposite within our nature (our shadow) and continuing, more whole and balanced, along our path.

The finality of separation can – like death – be painful and frightening for many patients or clients, particularly if they have grown to depend on the comfort of their visits. Reason may dictate conclusion, but fear may beg for a stay of execution and with that comes an inevitable instability which might confuse the therapist. Patients may try to distance themselves from fear of separation by failing to keep their appointments, or implying they hardly need the next appointment – a form of belittling the practitioner and their worth which can be hurtful as well as bewildering, particularly if a set number of final treatments or sessions has long been agreed and the professional is working towards the last one in good faith.

Again, we need to consider the power of the transference and counter-transference issues: the patient/adolescent is trying to break away/grow up and loves/hates the good parent who is engaged with them in this great transition. The therapist has feelings in the counter-transference which may well echo those of a caring parent: anxiety about the correctness of the timing involved; the firmness of purpose in letting their patient go; having to process any attacks without justifying themselves and resisting the urge to attack in return. Although this may apply more to mental health work, involving as it does deeper psychological subtexts, it is possible for complementary practitioners to experience similar dynamics with their own patients. This might help them realize why they may have felt uncomfortable about concluding sessions with certain people, and understand better what may have lurked behind their patients' unexpected, and possibly hurtful, behaviour.

Counsellors and psychotherapists sometimes regard their

clients' moves towards ending therapy as if they are adolescents preparing to leave home: not a once-and-for-all departure, but a slow separation from the safely familiar, one in which they may need to continue to 'touch base' several times before they reach true independence. This coming and going is reflected sometimes in less frequent sessions, when the therapist might encourage monthly (instead of weekly or fortnightly) meetings, or even longer drawn out times in which their client can experiment with self-reliance and standing alone. The same criteria can be used for long-term patients withdrawing from their complementary practitioners, when both sides are agreed that an ending is appropriate. Although a different timescale is involved, practitioners can still be on the lookout for fluctuations of commitment and involvement as they perceive their work as nearly finished.

An inherent ambivalence

Along with mixed feelings around endings in therapy, there is often also a sense of relief and an ambivalence about the final farewell. The client is free to spend time and money in other ways, and the therapist has a slot available now for a newcomer, freed from the burden of concern and partial failure each client always represents. Unless driven by hubris, that is, an inflated idea about the depth of their skills, no one can claim complete success in healing work. There are always doubts lurking: 'Could I have done better? Did I miss something important?' Ram Dass and Gorman (1985) ask the same questions and point out that when suffering is at stake and we have offered ourselves to its relief, we naturally have concern at how situations evolve.

> But sometimes this compulsive need to know leads us to doubt because we have a hard time coming to terms with the essential ambiguity of helping. Paradoxical and elusive, service is ultimately a journey into the unknown. Did we really help? Help at what level? We often can't find answers. And we don't know what to do with that. So we wonder, worry, turn off, give up . . . or just struggle bravely on, puzzled and burdened, wearing down. See the helper? He's the hard-working one over there, the one with the constant frown. At

some level this challenge is very plain. We can either be frustrated and worn out by uncertainty and doubt or try to find a way to open to the ambiguity, embrace it, work with it, be moved and inspired by it . . . and thereby come closer to the very heart of the service where true freedom is found.

(Ram Dass and Gorman 1985: 202)

Jeremy Holmes writes in similar vein, stressing the inherent ambivalence of endings which test our capacity as therapists to tolerate ambiguity, to cope with both optimism and sadness in the face of loss, and to hold on to a realistic appraisal of our strengths and shortcomings. 'Poised between past and future, every ending encompasses both hope and regret, accomplishment and disappointment, loss and gain' (Holmes 2001: 130). Holmes draws a cogent parallel between writers and therapists, suggesting the writer has to be able to let go of his characters and to help the reader with the inevitable feelings of sadness and loss as one comes to the end of a novel:

At the end of a good book we feel a similar mixture of regret at having to part with the characters we have befriended and satisfaction at completion . . . But parting is only possible when both intimacy and autonomy have been achieved. If we feel truly understood – found a place in another's heart – then we can tolerate aloneness; conversely once we have achieved a sense of autonomy, we can allow ourselves to get close without fear of engulfment or being destroyed by the other.

(2001: 131, 133)

If the patient has learned to tolerate aloneness, then practitioners too need to discover an ability to be left; time and again. They, too, must achieve autonomy and accept that loss in part of their work, for, inevitably, they become fond of certain patients (the relationship, nonetheless, being ethical and uncompromising), and feel a closeness which transcends the 'fix it' professional remit.

Accepting the fact of ambivalence around departures is another skill that professional healers need to learn, because lacking a robustness in approach can seriously deplete them. It may even be necessary for practitioners to seek counselling, peer group or psychotherapeutic help if they discover they are taking too personally the myriad of endings – expected and unexpected – occurring in their working life. There is always a danger that distressed feelings may spill over on to the next patient and inappropriately affect the session.

One homeopath provides a useful illustration of this. Zofia Dymitr told me:

> I was supervising a student, a man with a scientific background who was, coincidentally, uncomfortable around emotion. In a live session, I observed him greet his next patient – a woman – with obvious irritation, asking: 'And what's *your* problem?' When I raised it later in his supervision he thought he had said 'And what brings you here?' as a good, gentle kind of opening. What emerged then was that my supervisee's relationship with his wife was rocky and perhaps the woman sitting in front of him that day had somehow reminded him of the difficult marriage partner. Sadly, he lacked the volition to explore the dimension of his difficulty with uncomfortable emotions.
>
> (personal communication)

When the problem is terminal

The topic of death and dying cannot be left out of a final chapter on endings and never-endings. It, too, presents us with the likelihood of uncomfortable emotions, but all complementary practitioners are presented, sooner or later, with patients who announce they are facing imminent death or a poor prognosis. This can be shocking news and very possibly render the practitioner speechless, at least momentarily, while they grapple with searching for the most sensitive response.

It is important to hear such news calmly and acceptingly, waiting for the patient to elaborate on their story, or checking whether they need instead to be encouraged further by asking open questions. 'How are you feeling about this?', or 'I am wondering if there is anything to want to say about it?', serves as a good start.

We need to remember the wisdom of specialists working with dying people, such as the world-renowned psychiatrist Elisabeth Kübler-Ross. She says that ours is a death-denying society and that we hide it behind the sterile walls of the hospital and the cosmetic mask in the funeral home, but death is inevitable and we must face the question of how to deal with it.

> There is no need to be afraid of death. It is not the end of the physical body that should worry us. Rather, our concern must be to *live* while we're alive – to release our inner selves from the spiritual death that comes with living behind a facade designed to conform to external definitions of who and what we are. Every individual human being born on this earth has the capacity to become a unique and special person unlike any who has ever existed before or will ever exist again. But to the extent that we become captives of culturally defined role expectations and behaviours – stereotypes, not ourselves – we block our capacity for self-actualization. We interfere with our becoming all that we can be. Death is the key to the door of life. It is through accepting the finiteness of our individual existences that we are enabled to find the strength and courage to reject those extrinsic roles and expectations and to devote each day of our lives – however long they may be – to growing as fully as we are able.
>
> (Kübler-Ross 1975: 164)

Perhaps these inspiring words can help counsel a patient who wishes to talk about their fears of death. There are other viewpoints, too, to furnish us with thoughts to offer a dying patient. Alan Watts (1983: 129) has this to say: 'When you are dying and coming to life in each moment, would-be scientific predictions about what will happen after death are of little consequence. The whole glory of it is that we do not know. Ideas of survival and annihilation are alike based on the past, on memories of waking and sleeping, and, in their different ways, the notions of everlasting continuity and everlasting nothingness are without meaning.'

The emphasis always appears to be on living well *now*; that in accepting our death each one of us has a chance to discover life's true meaning by coming to terms with death as part of human development. Healer Maureen Leigh asks patients who confess their fear of dying, what they think happens to them. She told me:

> I listen and then say what I think, what people have told me as they experienced near-death crises. Invariably the stories are similar – about leaving their body, observing the medical staff frantically trying to save their life, of the light in the tunnel and the words they often report hearing, such as 'you must go back now, it's not your time'. I feel it is all right to break the rules in describing another patient's experience to my present patient: it isn't really breaking confidentiality, and of course I mention no names. But if someone needs reassurance about life after death, I do believe I should pass on what others have been able to tell me, whether in returning to this life after resuscitation or in describing what is happening to them as they go towards their death.
>
> (personal communication)

Towards life

We are living in times of uncertainty, fear and global catastrophies, both natural and man-made, *and* we are living in times of creativity, joy and progress. Darkness and light, like the Tao symbol where a spot representing each links the two curving halves within the whole, makes up the fabric of our individual lives: sometimes we rejoice, sometimes we weep.

Complementary practitioners, indeed all healers throughout the alternative and allopathic spectrum, are needed more urgently now than ever before to help ease suffering. We are increasingly aware that the *whole* person needs our therapeutic attention, and the holistic approach, central to the complementary ethos, requires that practitioners be multiskilled. This means practitioners should have counselling skills, a knowledge of psychodynamics and a grasp of the existence of other levels influencing mood, behaviour and interaction. Fortunately, the days are now numbered in which irresponsible complementary therapists can ply their trade without accredited training or regulation. Their lack of expertise and boundary-less ideas about running their 'practice' left, and leaves, responsible colleagues shocked. The future holds more regulation, better academic preparation and tighter professional structure. But this will also demand, quite properly, more personal discipline for those choosing to embark on a career in complementary healing. As Kübler-Ross (1975: 165) urges:

> It is essential that you become aware of the light, power and strength within each of you, and that you learn to use those inner resources in service of your own and others' growth. The world is in desperate need of human beings whose own level of growth is sufficient to enable them learn to live and work with others cooperatively and lovingly, to care for others – not for what those others can do for you or for what they think of you, but rather in terms of what you can do for them.

It is my hope that this book has provided some guidelines towards that end, and that the contents have awakened some new thoughts and insights. Let the poet T.S. Eliot express here how we may better understand what insight means, his words coincidentally serving to reinforce the mystical significance of the *uroborus* symbol introduced earlier in this chapter. Thus we learn from Eliot (1969: 197):

> And the end of all our exploring
> Will be to arrive where we started
> And know the place for the first time.
> (from *Four Quartets*, final section)

Could we legitimately borrow this beautiful phrase to refer also to the inner process, the world of the psyche whence our lives unfold as they are meant to, when our conscious minds are unaware of the nature of the journey ahead each time and we start anew with innocence and hope? I would certainly like to think so.

Appendix

Referrals and resources

Throughout this book, reference has been made to the importance, wherever indicated, of referring on patients to registered counsellors or psychotherapists. The two main directories which will be of use to complementary practitioners in the UK are:

The National Register of Psychotherapists
United Kingdom Council for Psychotherapy (UKCP)
167–169 Great Portland Street
London
W1W 5PF

Telephone: 020 7436 3002
Fax: 020 7436 3013
Email: ukcp@psychotherapy.org
Website: http://www.psychotherapy.org.uk

Contains a comprehensive list of accredited members of all disciplines throughout the British Isles, and some who are registered abroad. It also carries psychotherapists' ethical guidelines, which may be useful also to complementary practitioners.

Counselling and Psychotherapy Resources Directory
British Association for Counselling and Psychotherapy (BACP)
1 Regent Place
Rugby
Warwickshire
CV21 2PJ

Telephone: 0870 443 5252
Fax 0870 443 5160
Email: bacp@bacp.co.uk
Website: http://www.counselling.co.uk

BACP publishes an ethical framework for good professional practice.

Both organizations will have details of supervisors, listed geographically.

References

Angus, L.E. and Rennie, D.L. (1988) Therapist participation in meta-phor generation: collaborative and noncollaborative styles. *Psychotherapy*, 25: 552–60.

Anthony, C.K. (1988) *A Guide to the I Ching*. Massachusetts: Anthony Publishing Company.

Baker, R. (1995) *Understanding Panic Attacks and Overcoming Fear*. Oxford: Lion Publishing.

Balint, M. (1964) *The Doctor, His Patient and the Illness*. New York: International Universities Press.

Bloom, W. (1996) *Psychic Protection*. London: Piatkus.

Bloom, W. (2001) *The Endorphin Effect*. London: Piatkus.

Brightman, B.K. (1984) Narcissistic issues in the training experience of the psychotherapist. *International Journal of Psychoanalytic Psychotherapy*, 10: 293–371.

Capra, F. (1988) *Uncommon Wisdom*. New York: Simon & Schuster.

Clarkson, P. (1989) *Gestalt Counselling in Action*. London: Sage Publications.

Cosgrove, I. (1997) Taking care of the carers. *British Acupuncture Council Newsletter*, Winter.

Dryden, W. and Feltham, C. (1992) *Brief Counselling: A Practical Guide for Beginning Practitioners*. Buckingham: Open University Press.

Eliot, T.S. (1969) *The Complete Poems and Plays of T.S. Eliot*. London: Faber & Faber.

Ernst, S. and Goodison, L. (1981) *In Our Own Hands: A Book of Self-help Therapy*. London: The Women's Press.

Fortune, D. (1981) *Psychic Self-defence*. Wellingborough: The Aquarian Press.

Glouberman, D. (2003) *The Joy of Burnout.* London: Hodder & Stoughton.

Goodbread, J. (1987) *The Dreambody Toolkit.* London: Routledge & Kegan Paul.

Grant, J. and Crawley, J. (2002) *Transference and Projection.* Buckingham: Open University Press.

Groddeck, G. (1977) *The Meaning of Illness.* New York: International Universities Press.

Guggenbühl-Craig, A. and Micklem, N. (1988) No answer to Job: reflections on the limitations of meaning in illness, in M. Kidel and S. Rowe-Leetes (eds) *Meaning of Illness.* London: Routledge.

Hawkins, P. and Shohet, R. (2000) *Supervision in the Helping Professions.* Buckingham: Open University Press.

Hay, L. (1984) *You Can Heal Your Life.* London: Eden Grove.

Heckler, R.S. (1984) *The Anatomy of Change: East/West Approaches to Body/Mind Therapy.* Boston, MA: Shambhala.

Hillman, J. (1996) *The Soul's Code.* London: Bantam Books.

Holmes, J. (2001) Endings in psychotherapy, *The Search for the Secure Base.* Hove: Brunner–Routledge.

Kübler-Ross, E. (1975) *Death the Final Stage of Growth.* Englewood Cliffs, NJ: Prentice-Hall.

Lorius, C. (2001) *Homeopathy for the Soul: Ways to Emotional Healing.* London: Thorsons.

Lowen, A. (1958) *The Language of the Body.* New York: Collier.

Mackintosh, E. (1981) Exploring homeopathy and modern psychotherapy – Part 1. *The Homeopath,* 2(2): 55–63.

McLeod, J. (1998) *An Introduction to Counselling.* Buckingham: Open University Press.

McNeely, D.A. (1987) *Touching: Body Therapy and Depth Psychology.* Toronto: Inner City Books.

Millenson, J.R. (1995) *Mind Matters: Psychological Medicine in Holistic Practice.* Seattle: Eastland Press.

Mindell, A. (1982) *Dreambody.* New York: Arkana.

Mitchell, A. and Cormack, M. (1998) *The Therapeutic Relationship in Complementary Health Care.* Edinburgh: Churchill Livingstone.

Moss, R. (1981) *The I that is We.* Berkeley, CA: Celestial Arts.

Myss, C. (2001) *Sacred Contracts.* London: Bantam Books.

Naish, J. (2004) Appliance of science, *The Times, Body and Soul* section, 10 January.

Owen, G. (2003) New army of counsellors puts Britain on the couch, *The Times,* 13 October.

Peerbhoy, D. (2002) *Evaluation of a Community Approach to Healthcare: Catch On.* Institute for Health, Liverpool John Moores University.

Perera, S. (1981) *Descent to the Goddess: A Way of Initiation for Women.* Toronto: Inner City Books.

Pietroni, P. (1986) *Holistic Living*. London: J.M. Dent and Sons.

Pirani, A. (1988) *The Absent Father: Crisis and Creativity*. London: Arkana.

Rachman, S. (1980) Emotional processing. *Behaviour Research and Therapy*, 18: 51–60.

Ram Dass and Gorman, P. (1985) *How Can I Help?* London: Rider.

Rioch, M.J., Coulter, W.R. and Weinberger, D.M. (1976) *Dialogues for Therapists*. San Francisco: Jossey Bass.

Rogers, C. (1961) *On Becoming a Person*. Boston, MA: Houghton-Mifflin.

Rowan, J. (1983) *The Reality Game*. London: Routledge & Kegan Paul.

Rowan, J. and Jacobs, M. (2002) *The Therapist's Use of Self*. Buckingham: Open University Press.

Samuels, A. (2003) Foreword to N. Totton *Body Psychotherapy: An Introduction*. Maidenhead: Open University Press.

Shealy, C. and Myss, C. (1988) *The Creation of Health*. Walpole, NH: Stillpoint.

Shilling, C. (1993) *The Body and Social Theory*. London: Sage.

Skevington, S. (1995) *Psychology of Pain*. Chichester: Wiley.

Skynner, R. and Cleese, J. (1983) *Families and How to Survive Them*. London: Methuen.

Suedfeld P. (1984) Subtractive placebo. *Behavioural Research and Therapy*, 22.

Totton, N. (2003) *Body Psychotherapy: An Introduction*. Maidenhead: Open University Press.

Walker, M. and Jacobs, M. (2004) *Supervision: Questions and Answers for Counsellors and Therapists*. London: Whurr Publishers.

Watts, A. (1983) *The Wisdom of Insecurity*. London: Rider.

Index

Related books from Open University Press

Purchase from www.openup.co.uk or order through your local bookseller

---

COUNSELLING SKILLS FOR NURSES, MIDWIVES AND HEALTH VISITORS

Dawn Freshwater

Counselling is a diverse activity and there are an increasing number of people who find themselves using counselling skills, not least those in the caring professions. There is a great deal of scope in using counselling skills to promote health in the everyday encounters that nurses have with their patients. The emphasis on care in the community and empowerment of patients through consumer involvement means that nurses are engaged in providing support and help to people to change behaviours.

Community nurses often find themselves in situations that require in-depth listening and responding skills: for example, in helping people come to terms with chronic illness, disability and bereavement. Midwives are usually the first port of call for those parents who have experienced miscarriages, bereavements, or are coping with decisions involving the potential for genetic abnormalities. Similarly, health visitors are in a valuable position to provide counselling regarding the immunization and health of the young infant. These practitioners have to cope not only with new and diverse illnesses, for example HIV and AIDS, but also with such policy initiatives as the National Service Framework for Mental Health and their implications.

This book examines contemporary developments in nursing and health care in relation to the fundamental philosophy of counselling, the practicalities of counselling and relevant theoretical underpinnings. Whilst the text is predominantly aimed at nurses, midwives and health visitors, it will also be of interest to those professionals allied to medicine, for example physiotherapists, occupational therapists and dieticians.

Contents
Introduction – The process of counselling – Beginning a relationship – Sustaining the relationship – Facilitating change – Professional considerations – Caring for the carer – Appendix: Useful information – References – Index.

128pp   0 335 20781 2 (Paperback)   0 335 20782 0 (Hardback)

COUNSELLING SKILLS IN SOCIAL WORK PRACTICE
SECOND EDITION
Janet Seden

- In what ways is counselling relevant to contemporary social work?
- How do counselling skills integrate with social work roles and responsibilities?

This book examines these skills and their applicability, drawing from social work and counselling theories and methods using clear, practical examples. Skills are discussed with reference to social work knowledge and values illustrating how, when used competently, contextually and sensitively they can appropriately underpin good social work practice. Questions and activities for self development are linked to the practices discussed.

This new edition of *Counselling Skills in Social Work Practice* has been thoroughly revised to reflect the National Occupational Standards for social work which identify the importance of communication skills and a developmental understanding of people in their social contexts. The chapters are linked to the six key roles for social work practice.

This book builds on the strengths of the first edition, as well as addressing the challenges of practice in relevant legislative and policy contexts. The book includes:

- Evidence of how the competencies which underpin counselling practice are directly transferable to effective social work practice
- Practical advice on communication skills
- Examples of how to build effective working relationships; a whole chapter is now devoted to the specific skills required for working within inter-agency and multi-disciplinary teams

This book is key reading on the subject of ethical and effective social work for those teaching, studying or practising in the field.

Contents
Preface – Counselling skills and social work: a relationship – Counselling skills for communication – Assessing: relevant counselling skills – Planning, acting and providing a service: relevant counselling skills – Supporting service user choice and advocacy: relevant counselling skills – Managing risk and working together: relevant counselling skills – Practice within organizations: relevant counselling skills – Developing professional competence: relevant counselling skills – References – Index.

192pp   0 335 21649 8 (Paperback)

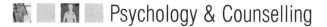